100 Days of Hell

Teaching A Struggling Class In A Failing System

100 Days of Hell

Teaching A Struggling Class In A Failing System

Nzinga Felix, M.ED

Published by He & Her Publishing, LLC

Atlanta, Georgia

The author gratefully acknowledges permission to use illustrations by the following individuals.

Front Cover Art: Koozi Arts, LLC

Text Design: He & Her Publishing, LLC

Editor: Intelligent Allah of Koozi Arts, LLC

ISBN: 0-692-90870-6

Author's Note

This is a work of non-fiction. Names (descriptors and code words) are from the vividly cynical and expressive creativity of the author. The specific school is artistically referred to as HELLementary and can be any school under an oppressive regime. Specific incidents happened, while the names have been coded to protect the perpetrators, the events happened. Any resemblance to actual persons (living or dead), business establishments, events or locales is quite possibly coincidental and likely means that you were there. This means that you can bear witness that it is in fact true, in which case you have my utmost solidarity. We survived!

Table of Contents

Gratitude

It is with much gratitude that I acknowledge my family. Thank you, Mekhi and Arthur, for being awesome students on your quest for knowledge. Thank you for being easy breezy when I was high strung. I want to also apologize to you, for the time this aspect of my living has taken from you. Through everything that I dealt with, you allowed me to eat as much ice cream as I wanted and allowed me to figure my way through this. Even in doing so, I acknowledge that time (which I can never replace), was stolen from you. So, I honor you and I meditate on ways in which I can make it up to you. I love you both and I trust that you saw in me a true warrior queen (brave, passionate, vicious, resolute, strategic, anxious for justice and ultimately centered in peace).

To my husband, I realize I was difficult through this time. Initially, you, along with many others-didn't know the Hell that was taking place, the levels and the extremes. I think this journey helped us grow apart so that we could grow stronger together. Thank you for offering words of encouragement and support in your own way.

Thank you for helping me tie up loose ends; helping me dot my I's and cross my T's.

Thank you to my awesome brother, Intelligent Allah over at Koozi Arts, LLC. The design of the cover is amazing-thanks for putting awesome sauce all over it. (www.kooziarts.com) Your business savvy skills are impeccable. Thank you for taking the time to critique me, for seeing the vision, and assisting in making this vision a reality. Thank you for encouraging me to be more human, remembering that you knew me before this trauma. Thank you to my sister, Ahsharah (the best doula and herbalist ever). There were many days you had to remind me that my health (my life) was in jeopardy. Tough love! Thank you, Ashanti, my Zeta Face. Without your professional eye, I might have been in hotter water. You know, with my emotions and saying/writing exactly what I'm thinking. I'm such a work in process. Thank you to my entire community, from Little Rock to Washington, DC and here in Georgia…my roots are strong. Abibifahodie and PEACE!!

Sister Aje, you are like the big sister I always needed. Thank you for your advice, the wellness support and patient encouragement. Sister Kania, you are a ray of sunshine and so very resourceful. I love your brain, I love how you make it happen! Thank you to all the members of the Atlanta Community Wellness Collective. We truly are healing the community.

Last, and certainly not least, thank you to the teachers who assisted me in #Room113. Please know that there were many days where this school year would not have been possible without you. We made it. #HELLementary

Thank you to the teachers who endured-I pray the world sees your goodness. I send love and support to all survivors of bullying and workplace bullying. #BulliesThriveOffFear #NoFearNoBullies #TakeAStand

Prologue:

10 Things You Wouldn't Know About Me, From Reading This Book

1. I actually love children!
2. I enjoy teaching and watching children learn.
3. I'm easy to get along with and I work well with just about anyone.
4. I love my life.
5. My cup is usually half full.
6. I'm a bright sunshine-a ray of light…cheerful.
7. I don't give up easily. I'm a fighter (having gone through too much not to be)!
8. I experience extreme anxiety when I am late.
9. I am solution oriented.
10. "I have come to lighten the darkness…"

For as far back as I can remember, I was always surrounded by great educators and teachers. My grandmother, the woman who raised me, taught within the pre-school setting. She cultivated within me a lifelong passion for learning and helping along with an admiration and respect for the field of education. Her generous nature put others before us every holiday season. Being familiar with neighborhood families who struggled through poverty and sometimes drug use/abuse—we would make special platters and serve the community before we said grace and sat to eat. I remember, and enjoyed, being able to help someone else.

Little did I know, there would be a long journey that prepared me to become an educator. In high school, we had a child development course on our campus. Assisting in the pre-school classroom allowed myself and other students to earn a grade as we put into practice the theory that we learned in our class. From taking this course, I took on my first job as a childcare worker at the daycare across the street from my house. After leaving the child development course at school, I would work with the afterschool children and learn even more skills with children of all ages.

As I furthered my education, I continued to delve within my passion of working with children. I was always the cousin who took the younger cousins and siblings to have fun in the park or arcades. This didn't change when I went into the military. I was everyone's favorite babysitter and honorary aunt. I simply loved children and seeing them be who they are naturally. I have plenty of nieces and nephews, who are not blood related however the love is still the same.

In true educator fashion—my grandmother, long after retirement—continues to educate through tutoring youth within various school settings and community organizations. Retiring, doing what you love and volunteering all the same—I thought would be the way my life passion and goals would turn out. However, through corrupt systems and the need for leadership restructuring, I found myself wanting out of the very educational system that once brought me joy.

Chapter 1: Where Dreams Go...To Die

"I was moved from a 2nd Grade classroom to teach middle school science. This was the right of the principal. I was asked if I wanted to move despite the decision having been made in advance. Principal waited until I was on break to tell me that "The Board" made the decision, not her. Again, moving me was her right, but she was dishonest in her presentation. Trust completely eroded." ~T. C. (Illinois)

Going into my third year at this school (and I use the word school lightly), I watched the already low morale drop. I saw great teachers leave (some having done so in the middle of a school year). I witnessed extreme behaviors from teachers, administration and students—some out of survival, some out of reluctance and some with hesitation. I have witnessed teachers become the blame for the resulting behaviors of poor parenting. I watched an administrator cast her staff out, forcing them to fend for themselves.

I came into this school, to replace a 5th Grade teacher who left this classroom in the early part of the year. I was told she left due to disruptive behaviors, and actually applied for a job out of the country. Entering this particular classroom, I could empathize with why she left in such a hurry. The behaviors in this class were out of control.

No sweat, right? I'm a disciplinarian. I love these little people. Let's make metal meet road. It was an absolute challenge. I was encouraged, though. After breaking through to some of the roughest and toughest, I could teach. We rocked out.

The next year, I had the siblings of the roughest and toughest and they were just as tough. I had a handful of young ladies and very few young men. This was largely due to the male teacher on our grade level having taught an all-male class. I remember asking myself, are they intentionally sending me these rough and tough children? Either way, I pushed forward.

We began to manage with one another. Although there were a lot of behavior issues, I could teach, at times. I had several ill behaviors from parents, but we worked them out. It was through these times that I could see why the children came to school crazed. The parents, themselves, were off the hook.

Not only were the children accustomed to being disruptive, but sometimes it appeared that their behaviors were promoted by their disrespectful parents. One year I had a fairly bright student, but her achievements were overshadowed by her (and her mother's) lack of respect for authority. That is, until she met me. Because I didn't allow the student to shut down and demanded respectful communication, she began to open up to me. She accepted me as the authority in our classroom. Did we have our moments? Absolutely. But she allowed me to show a healthy concern for her and push her to do better. Of course, she told her younger sister about me, and probably anyone who would listen.

The mother didn't favor me too well. I have standards and I operate within my classroom efficiently. I demand the same thing of all who enter my class, parent, child and administration. One time in particular, I had parent conferences scheduled in which the mother and father of this student agreed to meet me and discuss the child academically. I asked the parents, just as I ask all my parents, to let me know if you cannot make it so that I can reschedule and/or get another parent in that time space. For whatever reason the parents didn't make the meeting or call to cancel. I waited for a fair amount of time for the meeting, which wasn't adjusted because I had no prior knowledge of the cancellation.

I ultimately emailed both parents separately to let them know that I waited for them for their scheduled conference. I asked if they would like to reschedule. The mother seemed offended that I emailed her and her boyfriend, the student's father. She threatened me and told me about myself in several different fonts, emoji's and disrespectful words. She further threatened me and told me not to EVER email her "man" again. Wait, what?

Okay, these parents must not really understand much about life. Not every teacher comes from "la-la land" to where you can just threaten a person and think that fear is the first reaction. I'm just not that teacher. Strategic, yes, but you won't scare me nor run me. That's not how I am built. So, I went to my assistant principal to let him know that I feared for my safety and was prepared to defend myself if necessary. Is that on file? Great. Now, I wish a muthafucka would!

The following year, the second daughter of this particular parent and sister of my former student, was in my class. I knew of her from the previous year. Given what I knew about the troubled family dynamics and dysfunctional home situation, the need for clear guidelines must be set. She knew who I was and I was prepared for whatever might be thrown my way. So I thought. What I wasn't prepared for was how a parent appeared to intentionally influence a child to be disrespectful and disruptive.

This student initially came to me with a helpful attitude and showed me how she could excel academically. At some point, I began to question why I hadn't seen the disruptive behaviors that I was aware of from the previous school year. Other teachers and colleagues frequently checked on me to see what I was doing and why the student had yet to act out. Teachers would jokingly ask me how I managed within the classroom with some of the students, knowing that several of them were known to be disrespectful and disruptive to the learning environment. These same teachers would tell me that they hated when I was absent because the disruptive behaviors returned. They noticed, when I was there, the students were well behaved (for the most part). I'd simply respond to my colleagues that a lot of it was tough love, setting a higher expectation, demanding their best, rewarding them for giving their best and swift immediate consequences for disruptions.

The battle wasn't always with the students, though. It was, a lot of times, the parents and the so-called leaders. For instance, reinforcing inappropriate behaviors can directly result in more of the same inappropriate behaviors. This particular student began to act out, seemingly out of nowhere. She had been a somewhat model student, definitely improved from the previous year. She had been my helper and go to student, for a lot of things, because I could trust her. Then she started to revert and I couldn't understand why. The student assaulted another classmate and the mother attempted to come into my classroom to see the other child. No, ma'am. I put my hand up and let her know that she could not come into my classroom and that she could wait for her daughter in the hallway. I will protect these children, they are mine while in my care. No adult will intimidate them, not while I am around.

By the time the suspended, once reformed student returned- she was definitely different. Or possibly just back to her old self. It wasn't long before we were battling for control of the classroom. I began to suspect that it had something to do with the encounters I had with the parent and possibly overheard conversations, which I can assure weren't from me. The parent had attempted to remove the student from my classroom requesting another teacher. I pleaded with the assistant principal that if this was the case, that the parent be required to have a conversation with me. The parent continued to avoid me and the student's behaviors began to increase. I chose not to give in to the student or the parents demands. I needed and deserved answers.

I later confirmed much of my suspicion when the mother and I finally met face-to-face in the assistant principals' office. She initially met with resistance and became quite defensive. As the meeting opened, it was made known that she didn't run my classroom nor would the student run my classroom. My assistant principal sat back and watched the exchange. As I stood my ground, the parent admitted that she "felt some kind of way" about her daughter not receiving an award during the honors program which resulted in her pushing to have her daughter removed from my class. After explaining to the parent why the student didn't earn the award, the parent no longer wanted to remove her child from my classroom. She noted that she knew I was a good teacher and she could see the difference in not only her daughter this school year, but the daughter that I taught previously as well.

At this point, we forged a parent-teacher relationship. She no longer avoided looking in my direction. She spoke to me frequently when she came to the building to deal with the behaviors of her other children. And more importantly, I had my student back. The helpful student who showed me that she could be responsible—was back and we were ready to learn.

I truly cared about my students. I think they knew that. Even when I was tough, I showed them that I meant business and expected their participation in return. I was notorious for popping up at a student's home unannounced. If I couldn't reach a parent and my notes home and emails went unnoticed I would simply put the address in my GPS and be at the students' doorstep before their bus reached their home. The students would walk into a full parent-teacher conference with my notes and their assignments spread out on their coffee table. My parents appreciated this and many times-their level of participation increased.

In my fifth-grade class, I had one of many students who attempted to disrupt the learning process. This student would "forget" to have their daily agenda signed. The agenda served several purposes. For one, it was daily communication with parent and teacher. The parents could send me notes and see their child's daily homework (if it were written down). I would request that the students have it signed and returned each day. I would award students with a point system if I did a random agenda check. I noticed that this student rarely had her homework, nor would her agenda be signed. I pulled her address up through the school database and I arrived at her house before she made it off the bus.

The look on her face when she saw me with her folder spread out on her mother's coffee table was priceless. Prior to her arrival, I spoke to the mother about the agenda, to which she said she didn't know was being used. As soon as my student—her child—arrived, the parent demanded the agenda. There was no backtracking for the student. The proof was right there in her backpack. Yes, the assignments were written down but there were several notes from me asking why was it not being signed. The parent was very upset and I can only imagine what transpired when I left. All I know is that it was signed every day from that day forward.

I remember a male student in my fifth-grade class having a similar struggle with homework and returning it in a timely manner. I spoke to his 4th Grade teacher and was told that the child was a bright student yet he lacked motivation. I motivated him quite well one day. I went to his house and spoke to his mother. I didn't make it to his house before he made it home, because he was a walker. But to see his face when he opened the door and saw his teacher, was absolutely invaluable. My encounter with the mother, who was in school herself, was brief yet long lasting. She listened to my concerns and assured that things would change. And they did. She was more visible and reached out to me quite often. Every time she saw me, she would embrace me and thank me for being involved and showing care for her child. Even after he was no longer my student, moving on to his middle school experience, she would stop by my class just to say hello.

In many ways, I think I enjoyed my home visits. Although students pretended not to like seeing me at their house, they passed on the message on. “Do you know she was at my house yesterday?” and “She doesn’t play, she will come to your house and bring your homework to your mom!” or “She was at my house when I got home yesterday and I got in trouble.” Point made and the word was out.

I’ve also stopped bus brawls by hoping on school buses when I knew something was going on. I’d ride the bus through the entire line, getting off to meet parents at the students’ bus stop. I’d take my time to discuss information that I found out by trusted individuals and the bus driver would patiently wait on me. More often than not, our children didn’t want to fight-but because they felt pressured to do so, they might just go through the motions. Some students trusted me to diffuse and deescalate the situations and often times I was successful.

I recall a day where one of the *strongest personalities* in my classroom tipped me off to an incident that was going to transpire. It involved her. I truly think she was trying to change and mature yet her school surroundings and her peers wanted her to be the same. I went outside to her bus and took action. As soon as I walked up the stairs of the bus, I began to ask the students to sit down. I didn't know that I would end up riding the bus, but it was chaos. I couldn't understand how the bus driver could function.

I met their chaos with loud structure. My requests to sit down became demands. As I moved to the back, I could see where the drama might unfold. I began to pluck children from their favorite seats and sit them behind the bus driver. I walked up and down the aisle removing any student that sat three to a two-person seat. At this point, it became real to them and they knew I was about business. I told the bus driver that this is how we will ride home today. I said, "let's go." A student asked me if I was riding with them, I said "absolutely."

No sooner than the driver was about to close the doors, one of my male colleagues jumped on the bus and let me know that he wouldn't let me ride the route alone. He watched the front of the bus and I watched the back. The bus driver commented that this was the quietest ride he had ever had with this group. No, there was no talking on this ride. It was silent reflection time. Everybody, think about your day and what you did great and how you can be greater tomorrow.

When I met with the parent, who awaited her child's arrival, I made them aware of what was taking place and commended the *strong personality* for speaking up, for doing the right thing and rising above the petty differences. As for the other child, I simply informed the parent of what was going on and asked them to speak with the child so that we could resolve the issue before it escalated. As far as I know, it never went beyond that bus ride. I am so proud of the students for receiving the lessons and the parents for being involved and taking action.

It takes a lot and it becomes hard when it feels that you are alone or unsupported in your endeavors to effect change. At some point near the end of the school year, I felt what I thought was an irregular heartbeat. After certain things ruled out, it was suggested that I regularly check my blood pressure. Every evening, I would drive to the local Wal-Mart to monitor my blood pressure. I found that it would be super high. I soon invested in a blood pressure machine. I began to record my numbers. High...every single day.

Striving to be proactive, I began a yoga certification course. I stopped eating meat. I was doing yoga every day. Oddly, my numbers remained high. I could only come to the conclusion that it has to be stress. My logic was that I was doing my part yet nothing was working. It has to be stress. Okay, so by the end of the school year, I wasn't sure that I would come back. I truly felt that I had had enough.

I cleaned out my classroom, unsure and unbothered about what I would do the following year. My mind could only focus on relaxing through the summer. I watched my numbers over the summer and they slowly decreased. Again, logic, reason and deductive analyzing rocket science let me know that stress was the culprit.

Throughout the summer, I was able to breathe. I could relax. I began to feel better. I decide, "I'm going back. I can do this." That was probably the first of many mistakes—but it was a mistake that I didn't see until hindsight. A mistake, nonetheless.

I received a call from the principal, whom you will *affectionately* get to know as "The Cow." She inquired whether I would like to take the position of 3rd Grade teacher. This would mean that I would leave behind 5th Grade and the rising 5th Grade students that were known to be violently oppositional in their previous year. It seemed to me that leaving behind the rising 5th Graders would be a break or simply a welcomed opportunity to actually teach. Considering I had a run-in with a student dealing with the trinity of satan, its seed and its likeness during the previous school year, I began to feel that this might actually be my chance teach.

The trinity of satan, its seed and its likeness caused a lot of confusion with the young ladies attending the school. It was to the point that the trinity of satan, its seed and its likeness couldn't be corrected within the confines of the school. She seemed to run the school and no doubt any authority that attempted to redirect her. Well, I'm not having that. No person, especially a student, could come into my classroom and run me or determine the outcome of the academic day. I didn't pick with the trinity of satan, its seed and likeness, however if there was a moment where correction and redirection was warranted, I was not afraid to enter that realm. In doing so, the trinity of satan, its seed and likeness absolutely did not appreciate me.

There was a time where some of my students were at odds with this 4th Grader. After speaking to the young ladies in my class, I discouraged (and even "dared") them from engaging in certain behaviors with the trinity of satan, its seed and its likeness and her clique. During outside time, the trinity of satan, its seed and its likeness began to boldly approach me and my students. The audacity, right?

I took that time to correct and redirect. I began to speak to the students asking them who they admired, and who they felt were their role models. I began to speak to the students who were receptive to me. I asked the girls to look at their behaviors and see if they were in alignment with what their role models would do and what their role models stood for. The receptive students agreed that their behaviors were not in alignment with what they say they want for themselves.

As I began to pour into the girls with positive conversations and sharing with them what I knew about them—they began to really talk to me. Because the trinity of satan, its seed and its likeness became upset with the attention that her friends gave to the conversation, she stormed off. I further told the students that they should focus on being leaders and not followers or at least look at who or what they choose to follow. By the end of the conversation, the girls admitted to not having any issues with my students and made a truce not to fight one another. Awesome…issue solved, right? Wrong?

The next morning, before class started, I received a call to come see The Cow. No problem! Well, I should have known there was a problem when The Cow couldn't look at me. She said that a parent had called the school board and was upset that I made certain comments to her child and that I now needed to write a statement. What? Wait, what? So, I need to write a statement about what?

I found that other teachers had been recruited the evening before to write a statement and two of the three teachers refused. I asked those teachers to go ahead and write the statement because I had nothing to hide. I wrote my statement and gave a hard copy to The Cow. I found out later that the trinity of satan, its seed and its likeness has written a statement or had someone write the statement saying that I called her trash and said that she would be pregnant before high school.

Now that I think about it, those are probably all true statements. However, I NEVER said that. What was pointed out by the other teachers' statements is that I spoke kindly to all the girls, I counseled the girls, I gave hugs to the girls and even mentioned to the girls present that I loved the trinity of satan, its seed and its likeness, and when she was ready I would have a hug for her as well. So how did all this get twisted? Oh, I forgot, the trinity of satan, its seed and its likeness runs this school and The Cow is afraid of parents. Hell, she is afraid of the students.

After writing my statement and the teachers sending their statements (some for a second time because The Cow claimed that they were "lost"), I moved on with my life. There was no need to be worried, especially when I stood on truth that I never said anything unkind to those children. The school year ended and there was no other mention of the allegations.

Back to me being offered the 3rd Grade position. I received the call and The Cow was suggesting that my move to 3rd Grade would be good for me so that I didn't have to worry about "the incident." I don't know what "the incident" was all about, but I saw it as an opportunity to not have a misunderstanding with the trinity of satan, its seed and its likeness. Great! I accepted the offer two weeks before teachers were scheduled back. I began shopping for my classroom and what seemed to be a new beginning.

Within a week, I was called and told that the 3rd Grade position was promised to a new teacher and if I would consider teaching 5th. Hell nah. I didn't want to consider it. I didn't say that but I did say that I had my mind set on 3rd Grade and that I wouldn't like to go to 5th. That was that, so I thought. I got a call from one of the previous 3rd Grade teachers that expected to return to 3rd Grade. Although this teacher was told that she would be teaching 3rd Grade English Language Arts (ELA), she was being switched somewhere else and would I consider switching with her. It would be within the same grade but I would possibly be teaching Math and Science. Because the teacher was who she was, I didn't mind the switch. But I made it known that this is a conversation The Cow should have had with me and it was my intent to bring the conversation to The Cow.

By the first day that teachers returned, all was settled. There was no need for a switch and I would teach all subjects in my 3rd Grade class. There were so many changes and so many new teachers. So many teachers had left. This was really a reoccurring theme within the school. Typically, the county requires a teacher to stay at their respective school for at least two years prior to requesting a transfer. The problem is, no one stayed (or desired to stay) longer than the mandatory minimum.

Within the first week of students returning, I had set my rituals and routines. I was getting to know the students and encouraging parents to come in and meet me. It was starting to be a beautiful school year. By the second week of school, things were flowing. We were all set and more learning was occurring. By the third week of school, I caught my stride. Anyone could see that I was thrilled to be in this new classroom, with students who actually wanted to learn. I had my usual cheerful attitude, relaxed demeanor and an occasional spring in my step. I mean, I was happy and it felt good.

By the end of said week, the 3rd and 4th Grade team was called for a meeting. It seemed that I was the highlight of the meeting because my class would be split between the other 3rd Grade classes and I would move to another grade level. All of this seemed to be the result of a more than qualified teacher leaving 5th Grade to become an "instructional coach" or *Coachgate* where The Cows subservient minions are chosen based on acquaintanceship. At the end of the meeting, privately The Cow suggested that I would be moving to 5th Grade and that the trinity of satan, its seed and its likeness was moved to another team so that she and I would not come in contact due to the previous year's "incident." Okay, so there goes that word again.

I called the principal out on her choice of words, asking her what "incident" she was speaking about. She tried to be secretive and suggest that "the incident" was me calling the student a name. I quickly let her know that I never called the trinity of satan, its seed and its likeness a name and that I had written my statement during that time and that nothing came of it and as far as I was concerned it was over. Well, this wouldn't be the end of *Coachgate*, "the incident" and rearranging my position.

In fact, that evening I was called to The Cow's escape room, along with one of the new initiates of *Coachgate* to which I shared my reasons for not wanting to relocate. I was told to ask another teacher to switch with me. When I asked The Cow to look at why a teacher wouldn't want to move (just like I didn't want to move), I was told to pray. This hypocritical snake was telling me to pray? You know, this wasn't the first time I began to question her relationship to the Most High. How can she be of God energy or God centeredness when she (The Cow) caused the most hell in this school. But okay-pray.

I left the school and was later called by colleagues asking me what was the nature of The Cow announcing over the loud speaker, whether a teacher wanted to take the 5th Grade class. What? I'm out the building, I have no idea. I really didn't care to consider her foolishness, I just didn't want to deal with any of it. It was stupid to me.

The next day I took off from work. I needed a moment. I learned that the 1st Grade teacher wanted to leave her class and take the 5th Grade class. Interesting. Upon further investigation, this teacher wanted to leave because her class was out of control. The students that comprised this "inclusion" class were out of control the year previous. It seemed that since the 5th Grade class would be occupied by the former 2nd Grade and now 1st Grade teacher, that leaves this hellish class open for me. I took another day off work.

By this time, I went to the hospital because my blood pressure had risen. The doctor gave me a few more days off work. Great, let me wrap my head around this and go back ready. Since the inevitable is that I am now a 1st Grade teacher, let's get on with it.

When I returned to work, I began the transition. I started moving my things. I had a half a day to move my things and meet my students. A whole half of a day. Great! So, I went to meet the students. It was tumultuous. The teacher that was moving into the other class stayed with me to get me acclimated to the students and the routines that were already being established. She had a student teacher who would be going with her to the new class but I had a couple paraprofessionals that would be there to assist with certain students. Again, this is an inclusion setting.

Basically, an inclusion setting or classroom is where one or more students have an IEP and they need special accommodations that will be assisted by the additional support in the classroom. From what I was seeing, this classroom needed more than a paraprofessional. I'm thinking a police officer, a medic, a lion tamer or a priest specializing in exorcism, maybe?

My first moments in the classroom were greeted with a UFC fighting match. I became the referee attempting to break up one student from another. I carried the kicking and screaming student out the classroom just in time for The Cow to be waddling through the hall. The student teacher and I asked for help. The Cow seemed angry that we were asking for her assistance. I couldn't understand why—we are the ones trying to diffuse the situation. You do realize teachers have lost their careers behind breaking up a fight, attempting to restrain belligerent students. Yet, she appeared angry.

There was so much going on in the classroom that I couldn't wrap my head around it all. It was very overwhelming. Right after that fight, another one ensued. It was as if the energy shifted from one student immediately to the next. It couldn't be contained. We, three teachers, sat in class looking like we had no clue as to how to contain (and even detain) the students. It was a mad house. By the end of the day, I stood with my back to the class and cried silently.

Never had I ever cried in a classroom. Not even working in a Level 5, secured lock down facility with adjudicated youth, have I ever felt so worn-out. When I taught young adults from Washington, D.C. who were wards of the court and "sentenced" to a residential treatment facility, I never cried. I never wanted to give up. These same students in Washington, D.C. were expected to transition out of this program after having served time at a juvenile detention center for sometimes violent crimes. I never cried, I never wanted to give up. This same facility is where a student threw scissors at me for speaking life into her dark situation, yet I didn't cry, nor did I want to give up.

During classroom instruction, a female student at the lock down facility took offense to a comment that I made. We were discussing vocational topics where the conversation about being an adult was a segue into the topic that brought about dissention. Some students expressed feelings of being an adult because of the choices they made or even through the eyes of how the law labels youth as adults for certain offenses. A comment from a male student expressed that being an adult is not simply having children and he gave examples of his parents not being adults because of their bad choices. My female student interjected and suggested that she was in fact an adult because she had a child. I began to ask questions about parents and parenting. The conversation took a turn and became a dialogue between myself and the female student. I ultimately suggested that she was a mother but not a parent to her child because she has been in and out of facilities since before the child was born. I explained that she must find a reason to stay out of these juvenile centers so that she could be a parent.

I think she only heard me say that she wasn't a parent and this sent her over the edge. Before I knew it, a pair of scissors were flying at me. The student attempted to rush to the front of the classroom and several of her male peers stood up to defend me. By this time, the security officer who travels with each cohort restrained the young lady and escorted her back to the residential side of the facility.

I wasn't afraid at all and very much prepared to defend myself. What moved me was the fact that students began to support me and say that they wouldn't let anything happen to me. These are students that society wanted to write off. These students are the forgotten students of the streets—yet they connected with me on a level that was more than just I being their teacher. They loved me and I loved them. I wasn't afraid of them and I truly wanted the best for them.

After a couple of days, the student that threw the scissors sent me a letter of apology. I refused the letter and requested to go to residential side of the facility to speak with her. Typically, the residential area is off limits to the teachers as it was also a hospital wing. After a few attempts, I was given permission to go into their day room, which was like a living room for the students who became hospital patients after the school day ended. In the dayroom surrounded by her female peers, she apologized for throwing the scissors at me. With my psychology background, I processed the events with her and the group. We talked about what she heard me say and what I actually said. I encouraged her to successfully leave this program, never return and take care of her son. She received my encouragement and embraced me. I was never scared of her or any of them. They are me. I am them.

Now, here I was with my back toward the children who are expected to be our future…I stood—crying. Thankfully, the children didn't see me, but I felt depleted. I felt defeated and deflated. One of the paraprofessionals saw it and she immediately stepped in and tried to help with all the chaos. Clearly, this assignment, which was unreasonable and would create unnecessary pressure on any human being, meant that someone had waged war—and I was the target. The next day, I thought I was ready to start fresh, implement change and put strategies in place. It was a daunting chore. Before lunch time, I could feel my blood pressure rising.

If you have never dealt with high blood pressure, let me help you understand how it felt. It feels like the oxygen is leaving your body and someone is slowly sitting on your chest. No matter how much you try to catch your breath, the pressure becomes overwhelming and simply thinking becomes a bit more difficult. You want to drink water, as if it will help but nothing seems to relieve the pressure. If only you could see what's on your chest you could lift it off. It seems as if everything is in slow motion and this added pressure is all you can focus on. It's almost as if every beat of your heart touches your chest and each beat is isolated to the point that you either feel or hear the heavy beat and sometimes both.

I requested a substitute teacher for half a day so that I could leave and go to the hospital. By the time I was to take my students to the cafeteria, they were beyond out of control. I lined them up the best I could and walked them to the cafeteria. This was only my second time moving the children through the building and in those moments, you would swear they had never been anywhere. EVER.

The Cow often hid in unused classrooms, turning them into her extra offices. It appeared that she selected these hiding places for several reasons. The first being that her desk looked like a pigsty. Books and papers were always piled so high upon her desk that one couldn't sit down and see over the mountainous stacks. She also avoided interactions with parents, especially those who might become aggressive. In her hiding, she wouldn't be seen as available and no one could access her to solve real world situations. Her office, located in the main office near the secretary's desk, was too available to anyone who might solicit her help. So, she hid. She remained inaccessible. Most of her day was ostensibly spent in hiding.

In one of her rare appearances, The Cow emerged from one of her makeshift offices and instructed my students to get in line. They didn't listen. Why would they? They hardly knew her, rarely saw her. After her reasoning fell on deaf ears, she attempted to chastise me, saying that I needed to handle this class and that they have never been this out of control.

Wait, what? Was I on candid camera or some shit? This was the same class that was constructed of every hostile behavioral issue you could think of. Her insinuation is the precise reason why her hiding is detrimental to the very needs of the school. Being out of touch with reality, she didn't realize or acknowledge that these same students were placed in a new teacher's classroom the previous year. In this classroom, there were several incidences of a student biting the teacher. At one point, early in the school year, I passed the classroom and thought the teacher was leaving for the year. The teacher informed me that she wasn't leaving but had to take down her decorations because a certain student would attack her and destroy the decorations on her classroom walls. At that time, I taught on the 5th Grade hall and I at least had communication with this teacher, even if it was to see how she was holding up for the day.

These were the same students who were in this kindergarten class together, called 911 several times to the point where the entire school had to be instructed to keep our phones out of reach of the students or unplug them. These were the same students that were barricaded in their classroom, by the teacher, so they wouldn't "escape," the same students who caused so many disruptions that they were seen as unteachable. Eventually, the teacher didn't return. Why would she? She remained in that classroom, unsupported, for such a long time. And, for The Cow to say, "they have never been this out of control." Really? Where were the hidden cameras?

When this Cow implied that this was because of me allowing the children to behave in such a manner, much of everything else became a blur. I remember her returning to her hidden place and hearing a loud BANG! Did this Cow just slam the door? She did! I damn near went after her. All I remember is having two teachers barricade me in the classroom so that I wouldn't fuck shit up. One of the teachers called my husband. This same teacher suggested to him that I needed to get out of the building because I didn't look well. I remember hearing the other teacher say it wasn't worth it and to not give The Cow the satisfaction of seeing me leave in handcuffs. I couldn't talk. I didn't want to.

I left the building after going to the assistant principal and letting him know that I needed to be out the building immediately. He looked up at his wall mirror, which was positioned slightly above his computer screen and on the wall. Through the mirror, he could glance up at those entering his office while continuing to work. From this angle, he could see me standing in his doorway. He immediately turned and asked me to sit. I declined.

"Are you alright? Sit down."

I politely stated, "No, if I sit down, you might think I am going to stay. I have to leave here NOW or I'm going to fuck that bitch up."

He asked me what was going on. I could sense a genuine level of care and concern. I stood there fuming, holding back tears. My face and eyes beet red—I'm sure. I repeated to him, "I need to leave here or else I'm going to fuck that bitch up." I was not in any position to stay and talk. I was in full rampage form and I had to go. I needed to be as far away from The Cow as possible. I had only made it to his office because I had two teachers who knew that I had been pushed to my limit. Had I not been lovingly escorted, there was nothing stopping me from dipping into her hiding place and really fucking her up. My colleagues knew that this type of plan was one that I might not bounce back from.

After gauging my demeanor, quite different from anything I have ever displayed, my assistant principal said, "Go, I will take care of it."

As I turned to exit his office, he said, "Fill out this leave form. I will take care of everything else." I quickly and quietly completed the leave statement, holding back tears and bubbling over with anger. I exited the building thankful that his door was always open and thankful that he could see beyond the immediate. I sat in my car and released all the anger that was pent up within me.

I placed my head on my car steering wheel, attempting to regain my composure. Everything was spinning. My vision was blurred and I couldn't breathe. I couldn't believe I was brought to this. I don't cry, yet my face was wet with tears. The more my eyes dripped, the more I released. I realized that it was me that was crying. Crying, for me, sometimes feels like a loss of control. Of all the things one can do to affirm that they have things together, for me, crying didn't symbolize that.

Yes, sometimes, I would equate crying to weakness. I learned that crying meant being vulnerable. I remember the time my mother told me that she enjoyed seeing me cry. It was then that I vowed to never let anyone who meant me harm, to pull that sort of emotion from me. Yet, here I was, feeling weak, vulnerable, afraid, angry, violent, confused, disappointed, sick and tired. I accepted it. I cried, I screamed, I cursed everything and everybody. Then, I quietly said "thank you."

I don't know what my assistant principal said to The Cow, but by the time I started my car and drove from the side of the building—I could see The Cow standing outside on the sidewalk near the entryway of the school. To eliminate the urge of running my car onto the curb, I left the parking lot through the one-way entry of the campus. I drove as fast as I could for two reasons, my chest felt like it was caving in and I needed to get as far away from the urge to do bodily harm to The Cow.

I immediately went to the veterans' hospital, the VA. I knew that going to the VA would reduce the three hour wait time that Emergency rooms seem to offer as their norm. I also knew that my body was going through something that I couldn't quite explain. I felt confident that my doctor would be able to explain my symptoms as they related to my overall medical history, which dated back over 10 years with the military and VA.

My blood pressure was 158/100, extremely high. Because of the language I used, repeatedly saying, "I'm going to fuck that bitch up," I had to see a psychiatrist. What? I only said I wanted to fuck that bitch up. Oh, and I meant it. Of course they wanted to know how, when and all that jazz. I will let y'all ponder on that. But for now, just know that's where my mind was.

The nurse spoke to me to calm me down, but it only made me angrier. She couldn't understand how a first-grade class could bring upon so much stress. I get it, in a "normal" situation, first-grade is usually the sweet, loving and adorable classroom where singing, dancing and hugs happen. Yeah, but this class was the opposite in that spit, curse words and flipped tables were the new normal.

After staying in the hospital for over an hour and my blood pressure slightly dropping, I couldn't leave until the doctor prescribed me certain medications for lowering blood pressure. It was either that or stay longer. He wanted to inject me with something to calm me down and immediately bring my blood pressure down. I couldn't agree to that, especially not knowing all the side effects and what the drug entailed. Send me the medication and let me go, this way no one has to monitor what I will and won't do. Because of the unnatural state of my health, I was given the rest of the week off. I needed to relax my mind, body and especially my heart.

Being off work didn't resolve the issue, I continued to anticipate it and it brought much anxiety. I felt like checking myself into the hospital for some sort of observation. It was a very trying time, an attack on the essence of my being.

Fast forward to me being out of work for another week. I returned to school feeling equipped to handle whatever was thrown my way. I greeted my students with love and I was ready to start over, with a different way of engaging my students. The oddest thing happened. The computer teacher, who is actually a slimy slug wrapped in what appears to be a female body, peeked her head in to see if I was back. Interesting, we had never spoken to one another in a manner that was friendly. Academically centered, yes, as in are you ready to receive my students for their class with you? Then the confused new teacher peeked in. Hmmmm.

Before I knew it, both The Slug and confused girl enter my room to watch my class and The Cow was asking me to step out of my classroom. She informed me that someone at the school board wanted to speak to me? What? What about? That's what I asked myself. I dare not give The Cow reason to think I was concerned. Not even one bit. As we are walking the halls, The Cow tried to speak to me, but it looked too much like she was trying to "escort me" out the building. I walked a bit faster, knowing that her size and low center of gravity would make the chain reaction that equals walking faster a bit difficult.

It was early. I entered the main building at the Board of Education and found out the person that The Cow said wanted to see me was actually Internal Affairs. What for? And get this, The Cow claimed that they had called for me. However, that office wasn't even open yet. She is such a liar.

After a few hours of them trying to figure out why I was there, me not knowing and them making some phone calls—they told me that I could wait for the person who's name I was given as she hadn't arrived to work yet. Great! Being prepared with my survival bag, I pulled out a book and made use of my time. Still on the clock, right? Cool…let's do this.

I finally was able to meet with the woman in Internal Affairs. We talked and she couldn't understand why The Cow called Internal Affairs on me. The Cow painted the picture that I left work without permission, or abandoned my position. This alone is grounds for termination. She took pictures of a classroom that appeared to be dirty and out of order, stating that I trashed the classroom before leaving.

Well, I showed my paper work where I requested leave online the day my blood pressure went dangerously high. I showed paperwork where I was admitted into the hospital. I presented a copy of the email that was sent to The Cow with the attached doctors notes and questions surrounding why I was unable to take leave in the substitute finding system. It appeared that I was being blocked from further taking time off work. I noted that the classroom that I was moving to was unorganized, because the day that I left had started off being my first full day in that classroom as I was moved from one grade level to another. As a result, the room was messy because it was in the middle of a classroom change during the school day.

The investigator at Internal Affairs seemed to understand the dilemma. Her resolve and suggestion surrounded my medical situation and sought to get me a transfer. She acknowledged that without the paperwork that I provided, a different picture was being created. I provided proof that the same information that I submitted to her was the same documents that I also submitted to The Cow. The investigator said that it was "strange" that the principal submitted documents about me abandoning my position and didn't submit the medical documents that justified me being away from the school.

The investigator and I spoke for close to an hour, sorting truth from the lies that were presented to her. She seemed concerned about my health and stated that if her daughter had come to her with these same claims, she would suggest that the daughter push to be transferred to another school. The investigator inquired about the turn-over rate and being aware of other teachers that had come through her office from this same school under the same "leadership." She asked me, "What's going on over there?"

I pointed to the paperwork and said, "This isn't the first time the principal has lied on teachers."

The investigator looked at me with kindness and said, "I'm going to try to get you out of there."

Deep down, I was excited and ready to move on. I didn't want to have to fight or be in an uncomfortable situation in order to teach. The investigator wanted to put me in front of the regional supervisor, The Cow's boss. I felt this was exactly what I needed. I agreed. I wanted to meet with her.

I spent over a week in the Board of Education main building awaiting a break in the regional supervisor's schedule. I refused to return to work because I didn't feel safe. This cow was trying to set me up in the foulest way and I just couldn't sit back and allow it to happen. I saw how she treated others and knew some of what she was capable of.

The Cow did not offer this kindergarten teacher a contract for the following school year, calling her "ineffective" yet didn't offer assistance when the children were physically abusing the teacher on several documented occasions. She lied on several teachers and implored the assistance of her trusted minions. Teachers nearing retirement, with years at this school under a different administration, opted to leave because they couldn't take the unfair treatment. A different teacher was not given any notice and walked into a classroom full of police officers, looking for a statement. It was known that The Cow had it out for this particular teacher. The Cow sent police offers to this same teacher's home when she couldn't get any proof after falsely accusing the teacher of mistreating the child. The Cow went after another teacher, after a known deceitful and troubled child accused a teacher of slapping the child in the face. This teacher eventually was cleared and finally left the school for another position. Another colleague was accused of throwing something at a student and opted to go to another county instead of being under the leadership of a liar. This teacher went on to become Teacher of the Year. Interesting enough, like me, two of the teachers mentioned above all served their last year in room 113, years apart. Room 113, the gateway to a difficult exit of HELLementary.

Sitting in Internal Affairs, waiting long periods of time for a meeting, I began to worry about my own transfer. It seemed that they were subtly letting me know my chances to transfer to another school were dwindling. Yet, I waited.

When we finally met, it was in the school in one of the rooms that The Cow likes to hide in. The regional supervisor, who is abnormally tall for a woman, came in appearing to get to the bottom of the mess. It was a lot of mess. In these moments, I learned what a cow presented for slaughter does to protect itself.

With all of the aforementioned information presented, she denied and denied away. She even denied calling me weeks before teachers returned to school, offering me the 3rd Grade position. She suggested that this was agreed upon while I still held the 5th Grade position. Oh, what lies we tell. I called her out on it. When she presented a lie, I emphatically stated that she was being dishonest.

The regional supervisor couldn't decipher it all (or didn't want to). She acknowledged that she didn't know where it all began, seeing as this was the first time I have been involved in something of this magnitude. She let me know that she recalls "the incident" and had decided the previous school year, that it was nothing to speak of based on her findings of nothing happening. She further heard The Cow say that I am a good teacher and also heard me demand that I not be retaliated against. I pointed out that I had never had a bad evaluation and didn't want this meeting to impact the remainder of my school year.

So, yes, I was staying, reluctantly. I was given another week to get my classroom in order and be the awesome teacher that The Cow admitted to me being. Of all the things that were said, the most important or the one that made me feel justified was hearing The Cow admit that I am an awesome teacher, because that *is* the absolute truth. Get this. For show, The Cow tried to hug me when it was all over. I lifted my hands to stop her fake embrace. I shook my head "no" and told her that I didn't want a hug at all. Oh, Judas, I see you coming. I'm so glad we both knew what it was.

The regional supervisor acknowledged that there was a breakdown in communication. Her remedy was that The Cow and I communicate through emails and in the event that we need to meet, that it be done in the presence of another party. She further stated that we should sign off on the notes that each other takes in these meetings. My question is why would one suggest these things if they didn't see one as being either dishonest or as being the culprit in the midst of hostile territory? Again, this isn't the first time the regional supervisor has had to intervene with an educator from this school and The Cow. The regional supervisor further mentioned that I would not be retaliated against and that she expected to hear great things about the students of room 113.

If you have never been in a school such as this, I warn you that you might not believe what I say. But I can assure you that there are a host of other educators (within this very building) who have been there, reached out for help and finally moved on to other schools and positions where teaching was the priority, support was commonplace and their dream of academically supporting students were fulfilled. I caution educators who have gone through these horrendous accounts. You might laugh, cry or even shake your head at what we have gone through in our building. I can only caution you because I am going to share with you what is real as candidly as my vernacular allows me.

"Stress at the middle school level was incredible. It got to the point where I would dread Sunday evening and my heart would race on the drive to work on Mondays. Finally, the Monday after Thanksgiving, I sat in the parking lot telling myself that I was whining and I could do this. My body said otherwise. My heart would not slow down. My head began to hurt. I couldn't catch my breath. I called my doctor's office to get an appointment. As I described my symptoms to the nurse, she said I could NOT have an appointment because she wanted me to hang up and dial 9-1-1. End result—stress. I'd never had an episode like that before or since."

~T. C. (Illinois)

Chapter 2: Diary of a Bullied Teacher

"Today, I had a break down and felt like giving up. This year I was given the task of teaching one class of Intensive Reading. Well, today, I cried like a baby because I became so frustrated and overwhelmed. I am reading endorsed; however, I took those classes almost 10 years ago. I never wanted to teach Reading. [T]herefore, I never added it to my certificate. There are 31 level 1-2 sixth and seventh graders in this class and there is no co-teacher. Most students are reading on third and fourth grade level. DI [Direct Instruction] is crucial but how can you possibly do DI with that number of students in a classroom that is so crammed? I can barely walk around. Three of my students don't even have desks. They have to pull up chairs to share a desk in groups. Only three students actually participate in the class and the rest aren't even interested. The material for the class is so convoluted that I don't even know where to begin with planning. I really just want to do away with it. There was only one training class that I couldn't attend because it was held on the day I was preparing my classroom for the new school year. I am on the verge of giving up my extra period

supplement because I cannot deal with this[.] [B]ut that is not an option. I need your help. I don't know what else to do." ~A.B. (Florida)

My first few official days in the classroom were a blur. I was thrown in with the wolves. Itty bitty wolves, but wolves none the less. I had to take many moments and figure out the best way to go about this situation. I had to buckle down and get downright stern out the gate. This is a different breed. Definitely not the average 1st Graders. Far from it.

Day 1:

This girl spit on a student today. Can you believe the audacity? I mean, these were behaviors that were documented last year. What a rough last year. But the audacity though!!

I found myself angered. I was angry because the act, in itself, is nasty and despicable. I was angry because I didn't know what I would do if this child spit on me. Really, what would I do? I mean, the rational side knows I can't put my hands on someone else's child. But that other side, yeah—she said she would grab this little thing in her face and snatch the spit out her glands. But handcuffs aren't my kind of jewelry.

Then, I felt angered because I knew I couldn't talk to anyone about what I was feeling. Yeah, I hear ya…how do you let children get under your skin like this. But trust me when I say that these aren't your typical Gwinnett County children. No-they really aren't. Then, the support within the school is not there. You mean, go to The Cow and tell her my thoughts? She already lied on me and lied to my face and her supervisors face. This Christian cow has no shame.

Day 2:

I woke up this morning like, "fuck this job." Defeated before I got started. Defeated before my feet hit the floor. A chore to just get out of bed, let alone the stress that comes along with what I put up with on a daily basis. Then, I thought about something I say to my students each day. “You can have a good day, or a bad day—but it’s *your* choice”.

Well, that shit was out the door before I could make it into the school doors. The rain, the traffic and knowing I would be minutes late. The crazy part…I didn’t much care about being late to work. I didn’t even care to be going to work.

Entering the building, seeing the assistant principal standing in the halls means The Cow isn’t at school today. Oh, what a great day it will be. If you have never worked for a micromanaging, unorganized, unprofessional, self-hating, messy lunatic then you don’t know what happiness I feel. You see, with her being away, the energy of the school is lifted. It’s as if that dark cloud is not hovering over the school. Maybe today is the day things can get done in the school. Just maybe.

Another meeting during our planning period? We meet so much that it’s overwhelming. “They” talk and talk and talk and we sign in here and sign in there. Just another way to track us as data. Another way to fake like things are being done. Nothing is being done. These children aren’t learning.

In said meeting, I'm hearing that The ESOL certification course is (in so many words) falling through. Then I hear that we will still meet during our planning period on Tuesdays and Thursdays. For what? I ask the questions no one wants to ask. "Why are we meeting in here when we can work in our classroom, meet in our classroom?" The response, a lot of hemming and hawing. If you don't know—say you don't know.

I mention that I feel as if this meeting is just to say that we have "met." Again, more hemming and hawing and wanting to throw out all of what they ("instructional coaches) do on a daily basis. But you don't service any children? You don't hold any real classes. You just talk about data and make us sign in saying that we were here. That's neither here nor there.

See, *Coachgate* has come to mean a position that one has not earned legitimately but through their willingness to sniff The Cows ass, be her minion, fluff the order of business to seem as though things are being done. The "instructional" coaches are willing to deceive their way through the school year and escape with having done minimal work. This particular "instructional coach" doesn't know shit. Instead of her just saying that, she's trying to over talk and talk circles around us—thinking that we don't see right through. This, my friend, is why I give this bitch a hard time. Cause she ain't shit!

Classroom antics: No one spit on anyone today. So maybe that's a good day. I'm not so sure. We did our morning meeting. That went well. You know, social skills training—Yaaay! We did well with our early morning bathroom break. Yes!!!

Then there is this one child. I swear this child is the Spawn of Satan. Has to be. I have never met a child, of this age, that is so set on being defiant. It's as if she doesn't care. I struggle to find something that she does care about. I haven't found it yet. I caught her telling another child not to listen to me. What the hell? When they say one seed can ruin the bunch—it's so true. My daily fight is so that she isn't influencing everyone else.

Day 3:

By 9:40 am, the Spawn of Satan was already on the "turn up." Its picture day, everyone is looking so beautiful, but I had already set it in my mind that I would opt out of the class photo. This isn't the way I want to remember first grade. This isn't the way I want anyone to remember their first-grade experience.

Something has to change. And quick. The "I want to learn" theme is catching on. Sweetheart is the child that the Spawn of Satan told not to listen to me. Yesterday, Sweetheart told me that she wants to learn. When the Spawn of Satan told her not to listen to me, this tiny frame and big eyes looked at the Spawn of Satan and said, "I want to learn." She was serious yesterday. Today, she was serious about those words. I encouraged her to continue to learn.

When I heard her face this spawn, I jumped all over it. Because, in essence, don't they want to learn? They do. It's just so difficult when things are in an uproar. It's difficult when the attention is going to the ones with the bad behaviors. This thing cannot run my classroom. We want to learn.

So, I focused on those that wanted to learn. I made it fun, interacting and simple. Of course, I had to kick out the Spawn of Satan. She keeps making choices to not follow directions. Blatant disrespect, lack of parenting, excuses after excuses. How do you break through to that?

Our afternoon was lovely. We worked on place value and glued ones and tens to our paper. Messy, yea, but we are learning. The sad part, someone has to miss out on it for it to happen. I'm so thankful for the teachers that assist me throughout the day. Because I have the inclusion class, its 3 additional teachers that assist with the class. I truly couldn't do a thing without them.

Another faculty meeting. It's our weekly Wednesday meeting. It was actually alright. We were setting up our school websites. Although I took the class last year, it was good to get a refresh. I became discouraged when my second page restricted me from opening the page I set up last year. With all the questions and confusion, I couldn't get the help that I needed. And of course, I really don't want to start all over. So, I will wait.

Day 4:

Today, not so bad. It's almost as if the children are getting it. We have been going over our classroom expectations, rules and regulations, non-negotiables and the like. Teachers have mentioned that they can see a difference. I don't know. Maybe I'm wanting a miracle-right now.

I actually had an opportunity to teach, today. That was quite invigorating. I realize some of the students are super low. It's going to be a challenge, no doubt. I just wish some parents cared more about their child's academics than reality television.

Reading comprehension, for my students, is like a foreign language to non-native speakers. Hell, reading is too. After my assessment, there are a lot that don't know the primer words. Are we going to be reading by the end of the year? You better believe it. I just need my parents on my team.

I found out that I was called "the good kinda crazy" by a teacher who hardly knows me. I'm not sure if that's her attempt at a compliment or what. Let me assure you of this one thing: I'm quite intelligent, I just play a fool on T.V. But please keep my damn name out your mouth. Let's not even go there.

Day 5:

TGIF!! Satan kept her child at home today. Things went alright. I was able to teach 2 of 4 lessons today. That felt good. I'm working to get my centers up and running so that we can be more interactive in the classroom.

We worked on social skills and did a lot of assessments. It's amazing how many of the children don't know their kindergarten sight words. It's even more amazing how many parents seem to have not worked with their children, AT ALL. How can you be okay with your child not knowing what they need to know? I mean, one child didn't know his last name. Another has not one clue about letter recognition-let along the sounds of those letters. This is first grade for crying out loud. What the hell???

I have decided that I am sending a letter home to the parents to (in my mind) hold them accountable and ask them to do better.

We will see who gets rubbed the wrong way. Defensive is the way of the guilty. I mean, “hit dogs do holler.” So I’ve been told.

The day actually went well, aside from my low energy. I was pooped. I look forward to the weekend so that I can relax and do much of nothing. Well, I do have to create more centers, so I guess I will do something. But relaxing is my number one priority.

Day 6:

I feel like I am spiraling into an abyss of I don't give a fuckness. I woke up feeling like the life is being sucked out of me. I hate waking up dreading getting up, dreading going to my job, dreading the thought of working with these "children." Then, I pull up (late) and see The Cows’ car parked in the front and I dreaded knowing that she would be at work.

These children are out of control. It’s difficult to teach with certain out of control individuals. I mean, it’s like night and day when the Spawn of Satan isn't lurking about. She is already pulled out for a few subjects and you can see the difference when she isn't in the classroom. Seriously.

During a cutting activity, the Spawn of Satan is trying to cut others. She refuses to relinquish the scissors and has to be talked to in such a way to help her understand her ways. It doesn't work. She goes back to doing the same thing. It’s like she wants you to yell and choke her up. We are not doing all that.

The beauty in it all, I had a parent volunteer watching the show. I finally asked the parent to please tell everyone she knows what she is witnessing. We have three teachers in here striving to teach, one student throwing scissors, another throwing desks and whatever he can get his hands on, another student running and making all sorts of illogical noises. I told the parent to join the Parent Teacher Association (PTA) and ask anyone she knows to do the same. The difference in what goes on in this school and what happens in Gwinnett County has a lot to do with parental involvement, an active PTA and parents who won’t let this happen in their child's class. I expressed that we need help. We cannot teach through this type of disruption.

Day 7:

Not bad, not bad, not bad! The day was actually alright. I taught. Most of the children were able to comprehend. I mean, this looks like freaking progress. I can't even be mad.

I worked my centers and the children enjoyed it. Of course, certain key figures were not able to influence the group, so it was a pretty damn good day, if I don't say. Oh, but I do say! Fist bump??!!

Day 8:

What a day, what a damn day. I guess a girl can't hope for two great days in a row. Damn!

Oh, because "we" know that the state is coming in to observe, that's when we get on the ball and "clean up house." So, I was sent one of the "instructional coaches" to assist with getting my groups in order. A real maggot. It's truly funny (not ha, ha funny but funny as in side eye, blank stare funny) how people want to look in our classroom and say what you should and shouldn't do-yet have not one iota of care or true concern for the issues that plague your classroom, daily.

So, I was sent some assistance to help me organize some centers and structure the class so that we can minimize idle behaviors. It was interesting to watch theory attempt to be practice. So many of those "ideas" went out the door. Again, this is a different bunch of personalities…unrefined personalities. This maggot had no clue how to help this class, largely because she was thrust into a position through *Coachgate*. Bitch, you don't even qualify for your title, sit down!

I will say, I took from this experience a few great ideas. I will have to tweak it to fit within the parameters of what takes place in our classroom. I did notice, however, that this particular maggot was in and out and didn't come back. After dealing with some of these ill behaviors, a person needs a stiff drink. Oh, I'm so happy I don't drink. I would probably be an alcoholic. I guess comfort food isn't any better.

After school, I had a meeting with the Spawn of Satan's mother. She is so delusional. She claims to not know why her child is behaving this way in school and she doesn't act this way at home. Really, lady? Shall I burst your bubble now and share with you that I know for actual fact that your child behaved the same way last school year? Nah, I will spare you but I will not cut you any slack. Get the fuck out of here with that bullshit.

The meeting changed the students' accommodations. The Spawn of Satan now spent much of her day with the confused new teacher. Great! The crazy thing is mom fought not to have the Spawn of Satan taken from my class for the entire day. Truth be told, your child needs a different environment. But, since you are so busy striving to fight me tooth and nail about the irrelevant issues your child is being what satan does-evil.

Day 9:

Today was the first day that the Spawn of Satan spent majority of her day in another teacher's room. I must say, the day began so peacefully. We were able to utilize centers for learning.

Yes, there was still a hustle and bustle to assess the students with the leveled readers-but it was complete.

We had an impromptu meeting after school. I showed up late to the meeting and left the same meeting early. I don't understand how people (and by people, I mean The Cow) can spring these meetings on us last minute. I guess when you have no one to go home to, no life and very little social skills-it just happens to be easy for you.

Of course, talk is in the air about The Cows minion who has shared with various others that myself and a colleague are "bat shit crazy." That's funny to me. I guess when you don't follow blindly, and you challenge the status quo one can be considered "crazy". I will be that, but not because you say so, Dr. Minion, but because if that's what keeps you away from me-then so be it.

Day 10:

Although late again today-I'm looking at today as the potential to be a great day. I know that I have certain students who will be pulled out today and I'm hoping some of the rougher children don't even show up today. Shamed? Nope-not even.

One of my colleagues gifted me with a breast cancer awareness scarf and asked me to wear it tomorrow. I can't wait! I have never really been into the pink ribbon hoopla, however; I am empathetic to those who have been diagnosed, survived or even lost their life as a result.

My day started out with the Spawn of Satan asking me if I would like a hug or a handshake. You know this is one of our morning meeting routines. As much as my stomach curls when she is around and the thought of her hugging me, I loathe-I just can't leave her hanging. The love I have for young minds wouldn't allow me to reject her. I do teach my students that we can redeem ourselves, right? Well, it's early in the morning and she hasn't begun to act out, completely. So, yeah, we all need a hug every now and again.

I have this one student who is disgusts me. He is on a rampage by lunch, just noises after noises after noises. Right now, he is sitting outside my door crying. All because HE knocked lunch trays, intentionally, from the serving line and later out of the hands of other students' hands. What a day. But that's not even the meat of it all.

Some days I wonder if we are in high school, or even middle school. We have certain staff that operate as if they are silly grade school children. Case in point, Dr. Minion has already told about three different people (that I know of), that I am "bat shit crazy," right? Well, she has had two of my parent request services for their children. I'm not upset about that, as I am more disgusted that there is a lack of communication with these matters.

Everyone in the school is already stretched thin. To create more work on a colleague's plate-that's a conversation that needs to be had. Not only do these students need services, I'm in the process of doing that for more than half of the students in my class. It's a process. It's a lengthy process. When parents, who already haven't done their due diligence come in feeding off of your antics-it creates chaos where chaos already resides. So, I have to reign in this chaos within 10 days, federal law.

Great! Well, let's see now-who will help me? "Not I" said one instructional coach. "Not I" says The Cow who has very little understanding (or cares) unless her fat ass is out to slaughter. "Not I" says Dr. Minion…after I wrote a lengthy letter, carbon copying the necessary people. Oh, she's mad now. So if you thought I was "bat shit crazy" before, Dr. Minion, just know that its official-maybe even certifiable.

Day 11:

The day started with me coming in only five minutes late...that's a plus. I haven't been feeling it and I think it shows in how I drag into the parking lot late.

Greeting my students, I receive a few hugs from some lovely students. Awesome! Then the Spawn of Satan enters and evil eyes enters and it's all around chaos. With these two, it's like what the hell? I mean, they feed off one another. The moment you get one reigned in, the other begins the show. How the hell is anyone to learn in these conditions?

Day 12:

Today was alright. I mean, I will take it. Exhausted? Yes. Was there teaching? Yes. Successful? I would say so!!

Well, the day started like most others, except today I was only 5 minutes late. Kudos to me. I am striving to get here in better timing, it's so hard. I remember the days when I would arrive at 6:30 in the morning and have a full 40 minutes to work in my classroom. So hard now-a-days.

I was greeted by several teachers that I adore. We spoke in the hallway-uplifting one another. I recalled a phrase my sister would say while doing her "Fall into Fitness" boot camp, "A wall can be torn down".

You know-that's exactly what it is, a wall. This school and its walls can be torn down. It's been shown that this is what's happening. The state has pretty much come in or is in preparation to come in and finish tearing down these walls. The way that The Cow operates, her anger, her health, her condescending nature-those walls are being torn down. Someone built her up to be this miserable being, and those walls are going to be torn down. She can either submit to the will or suffer through pain. Those walls are coming down.

Throughout the day, the Spawn of Satan gave them hell. She showed out while the state was in the building. Interesting. Evil eyes also showed out, while the state was in the building. There is no behavior management inside the classroom that can help those "children." They need more help than can be offered in a general education setting. I just hope the state sees enough to make that determination. So we keep documenting, writing, hoping.

Tonight is our parent night at one of the nicer fast food restaurants. So we had their mascot in the building. One of the teachers came to my door and said, "The Cow is coming." I said- "Oh, she's coming?" The teacher looked at me like "what?" I forgot, that's my pet name for her. Oops!

Day 13:

"Teaching has become a secretarial position. I'm so overwhelmed right now with paper work." ~O.G.

Today was just weird. The moon was full last night and it showed in the behaviors of everyone. The children were out of control. I wish I could blame it on the moon-but that sort of beauty needs no ugliness attached to it.

So much is required in one day-it's difficult to get it all together. The school counselor appeared to have thrown me under the bus yesterday in her email. That resulted in The Cow sending an email at 6:30 in the morning, because she has nothing better to do. The Cow inquired of my lack of information at the Response To Intervention (RTI) meeting and then claimed that the "team" was there to support me. I hardly believe it.

Since I know that she is simply trying to cover her large ass, I responded. I included researched data that mentions that training and time is needed in order to successfully carry out the RTI process. I noted that her words implied that I had been trained, stating that I will be "re-trained." Well, in actuality, one would need to be trained properly the first time in order to be "re-trained." I see through what you are trying to do. Try again.

Day 14:

The Spawn of Satan hit a teacher today. Teachers are at the point of burn out, blow up and break down. This school, this environment is not good for one's health. The children are out of control and the leadership is scared. Well, at least one "person" is scared.

It's as if things are ignored because they aren't happening in one's presence. Children are allowed to be abusive to staff and are ultimately rewarded for it. How is it that a child, a six-year old "person" can hit a teacher and be allowed to get on the computer and play. What sense does any of this make? Where are the consequences?

All I heard was "the state is going to be here next week," "the state is coming in," do this, this and that "before the state comes in," Well, you know what? I hope they come in and see exactly why this school is failing. They need to see these children in action. They need to see beyond the fake smile of that Cow and hold her accountable.

At this point, I am just here to collect my check. Sad, right? Try working in this environment and trying to teach. It's sickening to hear all these people with little experience in the classroom say what should and shouldn't be happening. Well, come provide some examples with THIS class.

Today, I have 10 students from one of my team members class. She is out with a family emergency. I know she put in for a substitute to teach in her absence. From what I heard, substitute teachers have been warned about our school. It's not too farfetched-seeing as though I have had a substitute tell me that she would never come back to this school. And last year, subs wouldn't pick up for certain teachers. Sad!

Day 15:

I'm starting to get it. How can we expect happy engaged children, when we ourselves are unhappy and oppressed? I get that it's a choice-but every single day, it appears that teaching and learning is not the focus of this school. What is my role?

Having had my observation put off for an entire week-I was forewarned that it would indeed be today. The amazing assistant principal said he would be back. I said cool. I have my activity centers together and I'm going to copy another activity. So, with one temperamental copy machine for the entire school, I wait patiently in line. First grade planning period, first grade priority, right? WRONG!

Here comes one of the four "Instructional Coaches," (she clearly went through *Coachgate*) stating that she needed to cut in and make some copies. I clearly stated that I have an observation and that I need to get my work before I have to pick up my children in 10 minutes. This one states that she has to send something to the "District" and that it would only take a second. I reiterated that I had an observation and that my work was important. Why did this lady cut in line in front of me?

I just walked out the copy room. I sent an email to the assistant principal expressing how I was tired of being in an environment where teaching is not the priority. This lady called me and encouraged me to use the copy machine now that she was finished. I'm sure she only did this because she could see how upset

I was when I left the room. I told her that I no longer needed the copy machine and that it appears that teaching is not the priority.

Day 16:

I have become someone that I don't want to be, in an environment that cares very little about our children. Any time I have to use unkind words like "shut up" to get a point across-I know it's changing me. When I feel that I have to call people unkind words, such as "Cow" or "the Spawn of Satan" to describe the people that I am around...I need to remove myself from that situation. The biggest question is "How?"

I have to change my thinking, my surroundings and everything associated with it. In reality, I know this but in practice or real life-I can't seem to make the connection. Then, I come in this place and it's like everything I know is out the window. I don't like who I am becoming.

Day 17:

I'm not feeling it. I can't figure out what to do to make this thing work for me-even if it's just until the Thanksgiving Break. The children that want to learn-can't, because of the ones that are showing themselves to be unteachable. I never thought I would call a child unteachable. And so it is.

And the "State" is in the building, yet they (The Cow and her administration) won't parade them to the classes that are struggling, needing the most help. They want to pretend that everything is "All Good" when it isn't. It's not! It's just a façade for the moments that the big wigs are here in the building.

Meanwhile, I have a student in my class who the children consider disgusting, that is sliding on his back throughout the classroom. His group is attempting to learn something. Everyone is on task, somewhat, except for him (the garbage pail kid). Yea, I have become mean, calloused, angry and indifferent. I have to get out of here.

Then, a student from my class has torn the door decorations off another teachers' door. As he sits there, on the floor, kicking her door the only advice that can be offered is "[assistant principal] is in a meeting with the "State". Oh, someone please tell it. Please tell it!

I have to get out of here because I am being changed by my environment. First it was the stress and blood pressure. Now, its stress and meanness.

Day 18:

After sending an SOS out to my parents, via email-I only had one parent come visit the class to see what I am up against. I'm sure she has an eye full. The sad part-there are no communities, so she can’t reach out and share the information that she saw with her very eyes, to the next person. No communities, no support, a failing school and failed students. Just perfect! *sigh*

Well, today was a horror. My students cut up so bad with the art teacher that she attempted to bring them back early. The Cow was standing on the wall watching as the children acted a fool in line and in the restroom. The Cow told the art teacher that she couldn't have them in the hall misbehaving. I heard the interaction and opened my door.

I looked at my watch and realized I am still in my planning time. I grabbed my things and left the room. I needed to empty my bladder. As I passed by The Cow, expecting her to moo, she said, "Thanks". I kept walking and didn't even acknowledge her. What games are we going to play?

Upon my return from the ladies' room, The Cow was still grazing, same place. I entered room 113 where the Spawn of Satan was cutting up. Three teachers in the room and she is going in. I grab my copy paper and move toward the antiquated copy room. As I passed by The Cow, she again thanked me. No thanks heard-I kept walking.

This was early morning, 9 am behaviors. How about lunch time was no different? As I was picking up the children of room 113-The Cow called me to her pastures. She says, "Are you feeling well?" Of course she doesn't care, but would rather go through the motions of being half human, because it makes her feel better. I replied, "nope." I explain that what I am dealing with is more of the same, "every day these children are out of control."

She asks if her maggot could be of assistance. I told her that she had come to the class when they knew the state was coming into our school but hadn't been back since. The Cow suggested that her maggot would come assist me. I will hold my breath. (I'm being facetious). The fakeness and game playing were at an all-time high. The folks were in the building and now people seemed to be concerned. I was not impressed.

Day 19:

Because of last night's call to The Cow, which came in from a concerned "parent", there was a rush to help me get the behaviors under control. The "instructional coach," the maggot, came in to help me "establish rituals and routines." The Cow peeked in, initially. I was upset because I have rituals and routines in place-it's just that this environment is unteachable.

After I settled down, I figured this would be a great opportunity to allow The Cows' maggot to see what it really is. Come in, report back to The Cow what you witnessed in this classroom. Work whatever magic you possess and let's do it.

By the end of the day, five teachers are drained from this mess. The only thing that was learned, halfway-is how to line up, how to walk in the hall, how to go into the cafeteria and how to rotate in our centers. Did we accomplish this task? Not really.

The Spawn of Satan has touched ANOTHER students' private parts and the behaviors are pretty much the same as they are every other day. Random talking about nothingness, kicking, crawling on the floor, refusals to line up, running in the hall, off the hook cafeteria behaviors. The best part of the day was knowing that I may have some parents standing up to be heard. Parents are tired. Teachers are tired. It's time for something different.

Day 20:

I was told, yesterday, that I would have assistance from the maggot again for today. Do you think she showed up? She didn't. But what she did was tell my paraprofessional that if we do not use the strategies that she had suggested that we will be written up. Really? So I sent this email:

"Greetings [maggot],

[My para] stated that you made a comment in regard to "us" being written up if we do not use the strategies that you give us. I'm not sure what strategy this is in regard to, possibly the laminated poster which includes the "I Can Statement" and "Essential Question." However, the strategies that you suggested (with regard to the poster), when you came half a day about a month ago-was not explained. While I understand everyone is preparing for the State to do whatever observations they will do and things are being put in place now, it would be appreciative if there was more concern about what actually is rather than what can be shown to outside visitors.

I am doing what I can, taking every suggestion to make things better in this classroom. Am I not allowed to express what I have done and what has yet to work? If the goal is to help, and truly help, then the dialogue should be open to do just that. Please be reminded that these behaviors and disruptions pre-date my coming to this class. I am doing my best with what I was given to work with.

While I appreciate your assistance in the classroom, yesterday; that is not the end all. I have rituals and routines in place and yesterday you assisted us in reviewing them. The only learning that occurred (yesterday) was that of behavioral reminders. We have been going at behaviors and routines since I came to room 113.

As I mentioned yesterday and based on what you saw-if we are honest-you can see what we are up against. My certification doesn't allow me to restrain a child the way that you are allowed to do so. But again, that is just one disruption. Our hands are full in room 113- and I think everyone is pulling their weight to do the best that we can.

Any and all sincere help is appreciated. So, let us highlight what we have used rather than a write up for what we didn't use. That is, if help is the actual focus and improving things in room 113 is the goal."

Of course, I carbon copied (CC'ed) The Cow, the assistant principal and the paraprofessional that assists me (the one who told me). The Cow responded and asked that we meet with her in the parent room at 2:30 pm. I surely will, recorder recording.

The day was alright, considering we have some of the same behaviors each day. The Spawn of Satan was suspended for her behaviors yesterday, inappropriately touching a male students' genitals. The boy with the hearing aid actually did an awesome job today and I am so proud. I had a parent come to observe. I loved it. I need all the documentation I can get. It's challenging in here.

TGIF!!!! Let the weekend be awesome and slow, don't rush it.

Day 21:

Although I have been gone for two days and came in late today—it was a fairly productive day. We actually learned some things today, and it felt good to teach. I feel like I missed my students. Nostalgic? Maybe.

We had our weekly Wednesday faculty meeting. It was quite interesting. I guess since the "state" was here, The Cow decides she wants to have a morale boosting meeting. Our part-time counselor stepped up and mentioned, in short, that we have to find a way to uplift ourselves outside of the school. She mentioned that being happy prior to coming to this school, and work every day, is imperative. She further mentioned that we wouldn't find happiness in this building.

While I totally understood the direction she was striving to, The Cow missed it. From what I could see, she took that as a means to say, "just do it", as in do your job. Well, little does she know-we have some damn great teachers in this building. Many of them are run off because of antics like she displayed in this meeting. The Cow opened the floor up for suggestions and ways to improve things.

One of the co-teachers asked about bringing in additional people to assist with morning duty and afternoon duty. Side note: our co-teachers and paras have morning and afternoon duty every single day. Where, but here, do they do that? In any event, the co-teacher mentioned that the weather is changing and she welcomes the change of moving duty posts around.

The Cow responded with information from last year. She said, "Mrs. New York, I thought you were okay with being outside".

Oh, but why did The Cow do this? She moved into defensive in 2.2 seconds. The Cow further suggested, in a not so kind or fair manner, that the co-teacher come up with a schedule for duty. The Cow mentioned that she didn't have time to do the schedule and that she was busy with other things. She completely turned the meeting into a pow-wow of chaos.

Unreceptive, the meeting went on. Another teacher stood up and asked about having a level of support from the leadership. What did she do that for? The Cow went at her. The Cow told her what she didn't know, what she was unaware of, what she wasn't going to do and pretty much put the blame on her and every other teacher in the room. This is the common theme of such meetings. This cow doesn't want to assist us. She doesn't want to support us. She would very well like to see us struggle because she doesn't care.

I think a lot of people saw it on this day. After the many back and forths and blame shifting-I politely (kinda) grabbed my things and left. It's so counterproductive to even talk to her. She comes off as a know it all, and she knows shit.

What I have resolved, on my own, during my two days off-is that I have to get a grip on who I am and was before this mess. I love children, I always have. I am a fair person, seeing things as more than one dimensional. I am a teacher, an educator and I know that all children can learn. I am genuinely liked by people, because I am a warm and vibrant person. I have always been an optimist, looking at the potential of all things. I'm a fighter—I don't give up. I don't know everything, but I know a lot and I can find a way or make one. All of these challenges were changing who I identified and embraced in my life's mirror.

I want to be a great teacher despite what the circumstances are. I just want to do my job. At the end of it all, I will cover my ass, teach my ass off and let the chips fall where they may. I won't get the support I need, none of us will. But on the same token, I need to get back to who I was before all this. I won't be destroyed. She doesn't have enough power to do that.

Day 22:

I came in swinging. A great day it shall be, and a great day it will be. Even though a teacher is absent and I have part of her class- it will be a great day. I am that great of a teacher.

We did some unconventional things today. Well, not necessarily unconventional things-just some different things from our "normal" routine. The children liked it, they actually liked it. I am striving to figure out how this will be incorporated into our daily routine.

I am so thankful for the assistance I have in this classroom. We are a strong group of women. We are on point. We can do this! And we will.

Day 23:

A challenging day, yet manageable. My co-teacher was out, the Spawn of Satan in, guests on board-yet we made it. There was a lot of shifting to be done, but we made it.

We had students from the High School come in to assist with work readiness and college preparation. It was alright. Of course, they didn’t quite know how to maneuver through this bunch of students. I can’t blame them because half the time I don’t quite know. I did my best to support them and allow them to do the activities they had for the students. It was a welcomed break. Still a task, but welcomed.

Day 24:

If enough parents asked the right questions and saw to it that those questions were answered without fluff and bull-we might affect change within this school. The sad reality is that not too many of them care. I'm convinced that the public school to prison pipeline is real. I see it in this school, all around me.

We are in an environment where teachers literally fear for their lives, livelihood and sanity. Students can hit a teacher without real consequences. In this school, children can behave like delinquents and very little happens. A lot of us are overwhelmed, overburdened and tired.

The lack of support is evident. It's evident in the many staff meetings, in the classroom, in the faces and hearts of once prided professionals. The war cry is "don't become a teacher." Seriously, don't become a teacher. Keep some sanity and find another profession. When did this happen-where teaching was not the ideal profession? For me, it happened when I came to this school.

Day 25:

I came in late today. An official late. I'm hoping to have some great news soon. I visited another school today, and the environment was warm and receptive. It felt good to be excited about going to school. Then to return to this struggling school, although still on cloud nine, I felt out of place.

Many of the teachers mentioned that I looked pretty or nice and one even said I looked refreshed. Amazing what a little happiness or excitement can do. I want to feel like that every day, all day and then some. I am awaiting some good news.

Meanwhile, parents visited the school to celebrate the upcoming "holiday." They ate with their students. Parents appeared excited. The children were antsy and busy. It was a pretty good day.

Day 26:

The anticipation of good news, the excitement of this one week break and not seeing The Cow in the pasture had me super pumped! It was a great day, just an anxious day.

The students did really well today. Of course, you have a few that just can't get right-but all in all it was a great learning day. I thought that I would be able to show a video, but we worked throughout the day. Who would have thunk it? What if every school day could be filled with this much excitement? Oh, what a fun place to be. Well, I will take what I can get, even if in small doses.

Day 27:

Coming back into this place, after a weeklong break was definitely a chore. The mind may feel rejuvenated however the body doesn't lie. As I approached the school, my heart began to race and my stomach ached as I pulled into the parking lot. I was annoyed to just see The Cow.

I offered nonchalant greetings to those that I am indifferent to. The Cow greeted me and I returned the gesture. As I passed by her, she called my name to get my attention. She said, "I spoke to...oh never mind-have a good day." And her smile lets me know that evil is real. I guess she thought I should hang my head low or be upset. No, not the case.

I am aware that she probably knows I had a job interview the week we let out for school. I am sure she is aware that I didn't get the job. The position was part-time and from what I hear, I interviewed well but the principal didn't feel "comfortable" moving me from full-time status to part-time status; which came with a pay cut. I wish people wouldn't try to think for me. I know what I am doing.

I would rather have less income, work in my field and for someone (a human being), than to be in a stressful, unsafe environment with a micromanaging cow that hates her life. That's a lot, but it's the truth.

Day 28:

Today turned out to be a really awesome day. The Cow was absent for the better part of the day. So, turning into the lot and not seeing her stock crate in its designated spot meant it would be a pretty good day.

In any event, I had a parent volunteer come assist with setting up center activities. As a class, we reviewed our sight words and did center activities that were pretty fun. We even went outside today. Yes, we went renegade and stayed outside for more than 10 minutes. The children earned it.

Day 29:

The day went reasonably well. We covered a lot of information and centers flowed smoothly. The Cow was absent again and I am really beginning to think that she cannot be in the building when the State is here. Of course, she sends her minions to do her work. There are constant reminders that the classroom should be set up as a standards based classroom. I'm looking around to determine where this funding and supplies will come from.

It's a lot to be done and there never seems to be enough time. We were told that there was no staff meeting today, in lieu of working in our classrooms. How about we had a meeting to go over information on core clicks. I just don't understand how they expect us to get the information down pact and use it on top of all the other things we get unexpectedly.

All in all, the school functions as it does, but we learned some things. I was very excited about that. I think, thus far, this week has been a pretty good week. We shall see how it progresses. At this juncture, we are about 12 days until winter break and 107 days until summer break. Yes, I am counting down already.

Day 30:

The fakeness is real up in here! The state is walking through the building. I don't much care. I don't think they are here to help us. It's some formality. Ain't nothing gone change.

We had parent teacher conferences and eight of my parents showed up. I am thankful. I wish more would be involved. The parents that typically show up are the ones that already know how their children are doing. They are the involved parents that respond when I reach out. They already know what their children are doing. The task is getting the other parents out.

Day 31:

I am worn out. Trying to complete holiday activities with the children, is a chore. It's a lot of explaining and re-explaining. It has completely worn me out today.

The Cow isn't here today, so at least we can breathe a bit. I am looking forward to this break. If nothing more than just relaxing and eating, I am welcoming this break. But first, I must get through this day. I'm drained. It's the simplest of instructions that my students have difficulty with. And with that difficulty, the task takes so much longer than expected.

Day 32:

It seems, the closer we get to this winter break, the nuttier things get around this place. Children are out of control, instructional "leaders" (and I use that word so loosely) are trying to tie up loose ends. Sign here, sign there. Yet no one is doing much since the State is done policing for the moment. Interesting.

Grades are due-blah, blah and blah. I'm not sure if we have part one of our two-part bullshit weekly meeting. I'm not going. I just need to work on things in my room and be prepared to have my grades complete by the end of the day. Why do we meet so much? Very little is being accomplished.

Day 33:

Today, I find out that I missed "important" information in yesterday's data planning meeting. How about students that are in the yellow should be RTI'ed as well. Where is the RTI specialist? We stay doing someone else's job.

Planning periods are always taken in order to do someone else's job. Today, The Cow wants to do mid-year conferencing with the whole of Kindergarten through 2nd Grade teachers. Really? This is dumb. Logically, how are you going to get all this done? It just doesn't make sense. This Cow is always behind the bullet—

unorganized and unprepared and now we get rushed to do that which is important. I can't take it.

Day 34:

I pulled up to the school thanking the Universe for allowing The Cow to retire over the break! No red car (the devil mobile), she isn't here-could it be that she IS retired? Welp, not quite-I saw her waddle down the hallway with that mobile cart. Ugh!

Anyway, this teacher work day allowed me to work in my room by changing the furniture around and getting rid of some outdated unused items. Of course one custodian swears he can't move the dirty dilapidated sofa chair that I sat out in the hallway. I told him that I have no use for it and it wasn't my choice to have it in here. I said that I would speak to administration to see what they want done with it. SILENCE!

I later spoke to the assistant principal and he said that it could be relocated to another classroom, an unused classroom, my old 3rd Grade classroom. Sigh. He also said that they can C-50 it. Oh yea? What's that? That's when they trash it. C-50, huh? Okay!

I know some people that are C-50....in my most humble opinion. This whole school is C-50. Most of the books that we use should have been C-50 a long time ago.

All in all, the day was great. I organized the room and got out of here at a decent time. I have a whole laundry list that I wished I could have completed but whatever. By tomorrow, I will be thinking I should C-50 it.

Day 35:

The first day back, with the students, after such a long break...what a day! It was all about re-training and re-teaching. Going over rituals and routines and then repeat. I told my students that I missed them-because I did...a little. Now, I am ready for another break. It's so high energy in this classroom, all the time. Today was no different. The students were anxious to come back and I'm sure their parents were eager to send them.

One of my highest performing students didn't return. Officially withdrew. I understand because if I were a parent, I wouldn't want my child in this place either. But it's not a move due to not wanting to be here, it was one of family convenience. Whatever, my highest performing student is gone!

I looked out onto the playground and the same nail filled 4X4s (from when someone broke into portable trailers before the break) were still on the ground. This place is sickening.

We get called for an impromptu meeting. During said meeting we were all but told that we are incompetent. All of us. This is typically how our endeavors were undermined and criticized. We were told that our RTI folders were incomplete and wrong. As a result, we were given three days to fix it. We were expected to go back to the data from August (five months ago) and correct our errors. Really? How is this warranted? It seems like an impossible deadline given and an attempt to see us fail, yet again.

The problem is this, 1) we (collectively) don't have the proper training to complete the needed RTI process. 2) we (collectively) do not have the necessary time to effectively do the process. 3) when we (collectively) asked for the time to do it, we were told that we have more than enough time. Such is the case in this meeting.

One teacher spoke up and explained that we need more help and we need more time. The Cow told us that we have time and should use the time that we were given to complete said tasks. I spoke up and suggested that she is unaware of the time commitments in our building. We have two weekly meetings (during our planning time) in which our time is being wasted by doing tedious projects and other peoples jobs (such as the data coach). I also mentioned that at any given time-we are called for "impromptu" meetings such as the one we are in.

Again, we were told that we have the time to get it done. This Cow points out yesterday, which was a teacher work day and having had time to get things done. She grouped everyone in the same pot (which she typically does) and shared how she was told that teachers sat in other teachers' classes and talked about Michael Kors bags and shoes. Excuse me messy boots? Why must you lump everyone in the same category? Why are rumors being spread as the gospel? Why are you and your minions sitting around gossiping? Isn't there enough work to be done? And which one of your minions aided you in this thought process, providing you with unsubstantiated innuendos to further aid you in your delusions? I, personally, wasn't in a classroom that talked about such things. However, I was in a classroom getting assistance from a colleague on how to restructure my reading group. Many of us did use the time wisely, cleaning our rooms because some rooms didn't get cleaned by custodial staff, spraying bug spray because we came back to an infestation, organizing rooms for a new year and new way of thinking.

Other teachers, who weren't afraid, spoke up. One teacher stated that she has been in the school system for 26 years, she is aware of the many changes with the RTI process and while she sits amongst highly educated teachers, she refuses to think that we are all lazy. ABSOLUTELY! Then another teacher mentioned that she didn't appreciate being lumped in with the whole group and if someone has made such comments about us not doing our job-they should be willing to come forward and point the necessary people out. She further stated that until then, the person who was creating mess should be considered a liar. Well said!

We had some amen's from the choir. Yet and still, we were dealing with a systemic problem. People in positions of "authority" who may not be qualified to do a true service and remain in said positions because of their connections. The system is flawed. This

---

school is flawed and our children are suffering because of these flaws.

This Cow should be put out of her misery. When is retirement? Where is the help? Why aren't the so called "leaders" acknowledging what's going on? I already know the answers. They aren't concerned. As long as they can keep cashing these six figure checks and their children can go to a private school or be afforded certain luxuries and kickbacks from their own name or labor-it's a redundant question. Why am I still bothered? That's the true question.

Day 36:

Tension in the building! So many seemed irritated and stressed. This cannot be healthy. Not for us, not for the children. How can we function like this, day in and day out?

After a long, rocky day-we filed into a Wednesday meeting to which we were involuntary participants in a bootleg yoga session. And I didn't wear my yoga pants. *side eye* So, we were meeting the yoga instructor, for the first time, who had come to the school through a county wide grant. She was introduced to us by the name she has asked the students to call her, "Queen". Absolutely not!

Lady, ma'am, I'm not sure if The Cow told you-but we are oppressed and yoga, today, right now is not the way we (I) want to "team build". This is no team. This, is a mess. You have entered chaos and as much as I like our form of yoga-I have absolutely no desire to listen to or look at you. Carry on.

And so, I just watched and became all the more annoyed. Some participated, some did not. Some heckled, some giggled, some just watched the time tick by. We want to go home, and still there are other presenters after you. Who agreed that this would be an hour yoga session, with no mats? I'm ready to go.

I left promptly after the "yoga" was complete and before the presenters began. We are contracted to be there until 4 pm on Wednesdays-nothing more. So, no, I won't stay beyond that. I have a family that I love, some other place that I want to be; which was far greater than this mess. This whole set up was an inconsiderate act that took little account as to the additional presenters, the time commitments of others and the "participants."

Meeting after meeting, foolishness after foolishness. This place is a joke. I've heard it called a psych ward and even a zoo. It might just be both—wrapped in one.

Day 37:

Complete and utter chaos! Teachers were scrambling to get RTI paperwork complete, with little guidance. The paperwork was due today and now that it's time to cover her large ass, The Cow conceded and found additional time to allot to us teachers. So dysfunctional. How is it that majority of the school is in error yet no one sees the systemic problem?

I was given a substitute teacher to come in while I take 40 minutes to go through my data. I had no clue as to where to begin. I asked the full-time counselor if she knew about the updates and corrections need, but she informed me that she had been left out the loop. I went to the group chair, she was unclear of the details. I asked someone in 4th Grade, she didn't know either. I asked the new teacher and she said she received help from someone else and was unable to explain the changes. My entire 40 minutes were wasted.

Are we freaking serious? I said forget it and began to work on honors day certificates. I proceeded through my day un-phased. I gave it the old college heave ho, whatever.

The part-time counselor stopped by my classroom before lunch. She assisted me with a thorough understanding that we were getting data from August, looking at those students who were identified as failing. With those students, we should see what interventions and data we could use to support them. I had 11 students (out of 22) that are in the red—failing/below average. Majority of those not in the red were barely above failing. Only 3 students above average. Wow!

After lunch, The Cow asked how my RTI was coming along. I simply stated that it was coming. Shortly after, my assigned "instructional coach"-the maggot asked me something similar. I shrugged and said I hadn't started. That was part of the truth. So, a sub was put in my room again. I was able to test students outside my classroom to begin the process.

I was asked what date I would put on my assessments. Are you serious? Considering they give "fed" time for tests, around these parts-I will be sticking to the script. Such is life. I'm already doing someone else's job. Let the shit roll down the pipe, on that one. Y'all have some 'splaining to do.

Day 38:

Today was a bit rough. I had an RTI meeting early this morning. Of course there is always a conversation about teachers who have not done their job and the lawsuits that can be filed because students aren't being serviced. Well, wait a second-I am one of those teachers. No, I didn't complete my paperwork but I am doing my job. What you are asking of me, ma'am, is not my job but the job of someone else. This whole RTI process is really a job (in and of itself). The people who are supposed to know how to do it-DON'T!

What good is there to have an "instructional coach" when they can't assist you in how to pull off this tedious task. It's too much for a classroom teacher to accomplish-especially without having the proper knowledge of how to do it properly. According to one counselor, as a school-the documents were 99.9% incorrect across the board.

I have gone back to AUGUST, acknowledged the students who should have been in the RTI process. Meanwhile, I recall that this was not my class in August. That's neither here nor there. But to have to do this task, without clear guidance is very odd and strange to me. It's a constant thing. The people who are paid to do these things aren't doing it. So it falls on us, the classroom teacher.

After school, The Cow called all teachers to the parent resource room. She expected all of us to sign off on our Teacher Keys Effectiveness System (TKES), which is like some sort of evaluation paperwork. The issue is that she expected all of us to utilize the one available computer in the classroom. What sense does this make? I left and went back to my classroom. I understand this thing, this Cow, to be a sneaky one. She typically waits until the last minute to rush us all into this signing process.

What I have come to acknowledge and recognize is that this is when she sneaks in her foolishness. So many times, I have fallen for it. Pressed for time, so just let me sign and go on about my business. Well not today.

While in my classroom, I read over the paperwork and there were a lot of things in there that didn't apply to me. To my knowledge, she added this to everyone's paperwork. Well, just great! I had a rebuttal for it all. You will not hold me accountable for something you or your minions have not shown or taught.

While preparing my rebuttal, I was called to the parent resource room. The Cow asks, "Do you have to leave right now?" which acknowledged it was beyond our contracted time. I replied that I needed to go get my children. But in my mind, I knew that I would be prepared to stay as long as I needed to complete my rebuttal. And I did.

Here is an excerpt:

"I am currently using interventions (per RTI) to assist my students who are not within the 75th percentile. There are serious concerns with the RTI process and with adequate training, I am confident that I can conduct the necessary steps to assist my students. With the assistance of parents and instructional coaches, I look to grow my students according to their level of understanding and as close to the suggested percentile.

I am unaware of how to properly access SLO [Student Learning Objective] data. I will need assistance with this task.

I have found that some of my students have scored well in Renaissance Learning however they have deficits that are being assessed through the RTI process.

My only concerns with the non-negotiables are access to appropriate resources. We use worksheets in our classroom to further reteach and enrich the skills we are working on. Some of our materials, such as the science workbooks, are limited in quantity and are in bad shape. So worksheets are needed to assist with additional work. We do not depend on worksheets but they are used.

I do not understand how to use the data walls and keep them current. There was an attempt to create data walls in preparation for the Metro RESA (Metropolitan Regional Educational Service Agency) meetings however the data walls were not explained and have not been maintained as a result.

In the comments above there is mention of supporting "students in the RTI process" however teachers are in need of assistance as well. We require thorough and consistent training on the expectations and the process.

As for the dates that I have missed, it has been documented that many of these dates were as a result of serious health issues. I have provided the necessary documentation to support the leave that was taken. I plan to be here for my students however my health is of utmost importance and I will govern myself accordingly and as needed."

Yes, she tried it. She tried to slip in a lot of things that did not apply to me specifically and I was prepared to account for that in my evaluation. These games we won't play—not today!

Day 39:

I have been sending out a message to my parents requesting composition notebooks so that I can get these students interactive notebooks and organized. After a few days of emails and texts, I had a parent come in and donate 30 composition notebooks. Heart swell!

Today was an alright day. We had a few students who were out of control. That's about normal for us these days. It's just tiring. They have come a long way from where they were, so I can roll with it.

There is so much to plan for. We have an honors day assembly in a couple of days. We have things that need to be filed in permanent folders. It's just so much to do and not enough time. EVER!

Day 40:

As messiness would have it...

I get a heads up that a student is alleging to her teacher that she isn't to be marked absent because she was in the front office writing a letter about me. The teacher inquires of the student, asking what she meant.

According to the student, her sister was scratched by me and they are now writing it up with the front office. The student explains that she was asked to describe me and how she knew that "I scratched" this child or her sister. The teacher wanted me to know so that I can be prepared for the shit that inevitably rolls downhill. The most interesting part is that I have no knowledge of the students in question. I have not put my hands on any child, scratch or otherwise. So I listened and acknowledged the heads up.

The teacher who brought me the information was asked, “when did this ‘scratch’ occur”? As I further comb over the details of this new allegation, I assert that the ‘scratch” would still be fresh (or new). I further rationalized that this child will need to describe what I was wearing, not just who I am. If a child sees me every single day, they should be able to describe me. But one will need more to try and pin something like this on me. *Please explain to me when and where this happened? At what point did 1st Grade teachers and students interact with 3rd Grade teachers and students, since we do not share any extracurricular activities or break times.*

My resolve is that I stand on the truth and it absolutely did not happen. I just look to the drama that The Cow brings when she gets word of things such as this. She is the messiest of the bunch and she thrives on drama. She can wait on it.

The social worker enters my classroom, with the student who alleged that I scratched her. The social worker pointed to me and asked the student, “Do you know her?”

The student shook her head no. The social worker continued, “You don’t know this teacher?”

Again, the little girl shook her head, “no”. I extended my hand so that she could shake my hand and I introduced myself. The social worker asked the little girl, “Is this the teacher that scratched you?”

The little girl, again, shook her head “no”. The social worker escorted the little girl out my classroom, turned her head to look back at me and whispered, “Thank you. Case closed”.

As it turns out, this child doesn’t know me. She was brought to me by the school social worker as part of protocol, I’m assuming. The little girl didn’t know me, nor did I know her. I couldn’t recall having seen her in the school, ever. Not even when I taught third grade for three weeks. Come to find out, this student was told to say that I scratched her, but she didn’t even know who I was, nor did I know who she was. What in the world?

Day 41:

Honors day...

Today was ridiculously chaotic. The assembly for honors day was just about everything we didn't practice. We managed though. I am just glad that it is over.

Since our honors day program was at 8:30 am, we spent the remainder of the day watching educational videos and playing outside. Much of the staff had been pulled to assist with the assembly. So this was an all-day event. I am super drained.

The "leadership team" came around with coffee and donuts and certificates for an "Outstanding Job." I welcomed that energy rush. Now, I needed a nap.

Day 42:

I was so close to losing my certification today!

One of these heathens attempted to spit on me. I reacted versus responded. I reached my hand out to grab that face...then I had to stop and think. I put my finger up and told the child with the evil eyes, "You gone make me lose my license." Then I told her that she could not come back into the classroom. I called an administrator (for the second time) and had them come escort her somewhere.

By lunch, evil eyes returned to my class and a brief conference had been had with the parent. The student apologized, rolled some tears out her eyes and it seemed we would be back to something like normal. What is normal for this sort of setting? I am so unclear. It's so chaotic in this building that what seems right is wrong and everything that is wrong is embraced, protected and fought for as if it's the single truth. I'm so confused.

Oh, after lunch, after lunch, after lunch—what are we doing? It didn't get any better. What are we doing? Regressing? Things seemed to be getting better and now—I have no idea. I was actually starting to say nice things about this class. Can I take it all back? Goodness.

So, this heathen cut up again. It was to the point that three "administrators" had to come get this little person. Evil eyes sat in the hall, screaming and yelling. She cut up so bad that I closed my door to silence most of the noise. I want the cameras to capture it all.

That is, if they work. See what foolishness we deal with. Then, I beg you, do something.

Mom came up to the school at the end of the day to get some feedback and see how the rest of the day went. The one thing I will commend mom on is that she came back to check in. This is a big step from what I had initially. This is the same parent that told me that she usually ignores the schools phone calls because it's always something bad, always something. This is the same parent who I asked to give me a chance and show her what I could do. This is the same child, who at one point I kissed her on her forehead with my heart filled with love at something wonderful she did. And now—today...we are back to being a heathen? Wow!

Today, mom stands before me and says this child doesn't act like this at home. Well, ma'am, it's hard to believe that because I remember your child from last year and I was on a different hall. Your son is off the chain and he comes to school so heavily medicated that when he is off his medication it's like World War 3 in this place. I have a hard time taking you at your word. Forgive me.

Today was not my day. I leave with a headache and plenty of frustration.

Day 43:

This cannot be healthy. This absolutely cannot be healthy. The anticipation of arriving at this place brings so much anxiety. I feel like my chest is caving in. My blood pressure wasn't high this morning but my chest felt awful. The same way I felt yesterday after the foolishness.

During a staff meeting yesterday evening, I was afforded a front seat at the insanity. A petty "supervisor" who was clearly unhappy in her own life. Cult like followers who refuse to speak up, rather going with the flow to hold a position that they earned through affiliation. The Cow just keeps mess going. So many indirect and condescending accusations. The Cow apparently thinks that the people who work here are either idiots or delusional.

A seasoned teacher made a wise observation yesterday. In our conversation, she asked who takes the heat for a classroom of students failing? The teachers. Right? Because it is assumed that the teacher didn't teach the information correctly or successfully and that's measured by the results of the student. So, who takes the heat for the teachers failing? Right! The principal. HOWEVER-that's not what happens here. We have (and had) some great teachers, yet it appears that nothing we do is right, enough or valued. So we, the teachers, are presented with so much yet it's not us. Has anyone looked at the high turnover rate in this school?

Apparently not. This school year alone, we have about 20 new teachers. Last year, we had about 15 new teachers, with more than 3 band teachers leaving and coming as well as 4 speech teachers leaving and coming. The year that I came to this HELLementary, we had about 15 new teachers as well. What's going on? Even in sports, when the coach is failing, they get rid of them and get someone better. Why has this Cow not been replaced? Friends in "high" places? *shrugs*

Point proven, when I hear that the computer teacher (The Slug) is walking around doing observations. I'm trying to figure out the justification in all this buffoonery. You have teachers who are now so called "instructional coaches" who haven't coached a thing. All they seem to do is rub shoulders, fellowship at the same church and maintain fictional friendships. What is really had is another comfortable yes "woman" who holds on to her job by cosigning us doing her work. These fictional friendships and "friends" in strategic places are there to accomplish the deceitful mission put in place by The Cow. These minions, slugs and lost souls are okay with the destruction. In fact, comfortable in it.

Day 44:

An early dismissal day for impending inclement weather? Talk about excitement. I don't think I have seen this many smiles since the day we were leaving for the winter break. Since we are here today, this won't affect our summer break or the inclement weather make-up day. Oh goodie!

The craziest thing about today is that the chaos never leaves. Where are the Standard Operating Procedures (SOPs) for any of the things we do? We all are just going off the cuff. Parents are frantically trying to get their children and its chaotic. Some of the nursery vans aren't coming to get the aftercare children...what? Why aren't there procedures to handle this sort of thing? Oh, I must have forgotten where I work. This is HELLementary.

According to The Cow, prior to us leaving, not only do we have to clock out with the key fobs but we also have to sign out. A signature. This thing is a micromanaging piece of work. And not artwork, you know the pretty art that you look at and see how great it is. Nah, she is a fucked-up mess. No wonder this school is going to hell in a hand basket.

I've been ready to jump ship.

Day 45:

While I know what I need to do, there is such a disconnect with what I feel to do or what I want to do.

Last night, I troubled myself with the thought of coming into this place. I had so much anxiety around just being in this environment. It was overwhelming and taxing on my body. I noticed that this is my typical Sunday routine. I dread going to bed because I know that I have to arise and prepare to walk into hell, the HELLementary school.

Then I also know that I can choose to not entertain the crap. I know that, but this is where the disconnect comes into effect. My mind, body, and spirit aren't in alignment. At this point, I know that I must fight hard to center myself. My body aches and the tension is all in my shoulders. My mind is cloudy because one moment I want to quit and the other minute I know that's not the best thing right now (today). My spirit is fighting to make it all make sense.

Last night, I received a text message from the assistant principal inquiring about an update on the lesson plans. I ignored it. I felt like it was too late. I'm too tired and really just unconcerned. Why are these changes being added to an already full plate without the proper assistance? Why do I continue to concern myself with the question, "Why?"

My husband told me that I should just make the needed adjustments. His logic is that if I don't, then everything The Cow is trying to say about me—that picture that she is trying to paint, will look true in the eyes of people that don't know. I'm so hard headed and stubborn.

My assistant principal came in to check on me by the end of the day. He asked if I got his text. I told him I did. He asked if I made the changes. I said I didn't. I explained that I really don't know what to do and that the help has not been forthcoming. The documentations are in place, claiming that we are doing things that we aren't truly doing. As a result; I have no idea what the expectation is. He said he would help me because he doesn't want me to be out there looking bad. Thank you so much for looking out for me. Truly!!

The sad part about all this...I have people in my corner that care more than I am willing to care. I'm being really selfish, to myself and against my own benefit. I'm going to meet with my assistant principal and get these lesson plans in order. I'm going to do my part. When the State comes in tomorrow, let them see the greatness in the teachers and weed out the micromanaging, life sucking "leadership."

It's a battle and I know that I must remain strategic and diligent. That's what warriors do.

Day 46:

So actually, the district was in the building today. It was a true horse and pony show for the people. The Cow sent her droves around to check and see if I (and maybe others) knew what lesson we were on. I actually didn't, but I knew the chapter and page number. Sue me!

The lady who came representing the district was in my classroom all of five minutes. She came as I was fumbling with the technology in this classroom. In our class, I have a promethean board that was very temperamental, working when it wanted. When it did work, the motor was loud, even against our imbalanced clatter. The bulb was so bad that you can barely see the projection on the screen except for when all the lights in the class are off.

District lady, ma'am, I hope you see this bullshit. I hope you write it on your clipboard that the technology sucks and the classroom isn't fit for animals. I hope you see exactly what you need to see and more. I am not afraid to show you that I am a great teacher nor am I afraid to show you that this is some bullshit! Write all that down!

Day 47:

A day what a day. I had an observation early in the morning. I was on some teaching type shit! So I'm good. My students were on point and we rocked out. I shall toot my own horn. TOOT, TOOT!

I found out that my students have grown academically since August. Of course, that's what they are "supposed" to do but some days, in this classroom—I just don't know. I am pretty excited about their growth. Of course, we are still working on social skills and striving to not eat each other alive, but we are making progress.

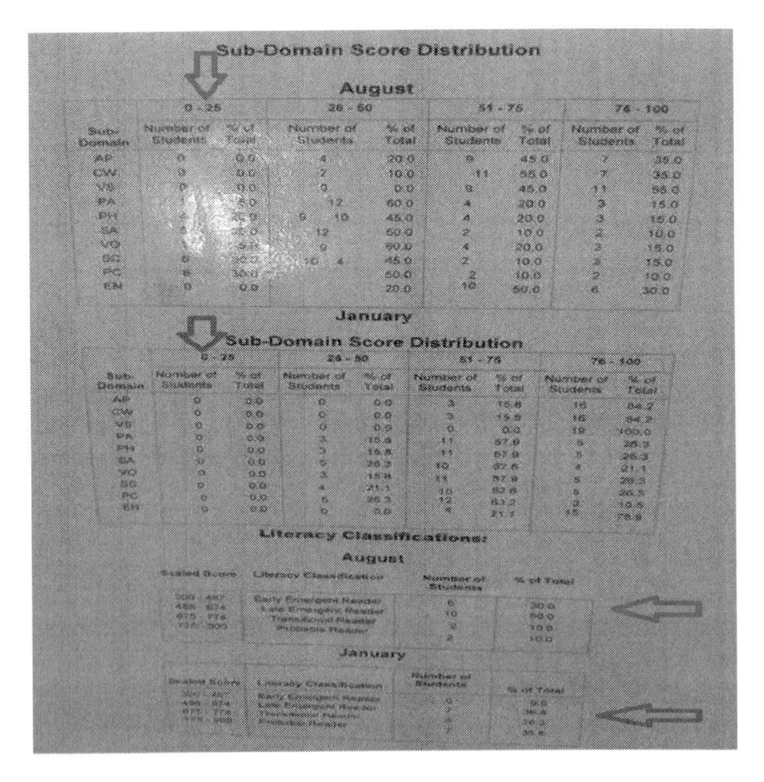

Sub-Domain Score Distribution

August

	0 - 25		26 - 50		51 - 75		76 - 100	
Sub-Domain	Number of Students	% of Total	Number of Students	% of Total	Number of Students	% of Total	Number of Students	% of Total
AP	0	0.0	4	20.0	9	45.0	7	35.0
CW	0	0.0	2	10.0	11	55.0	7	35.0
VS	0	0.0	0	0.0	9	45.0	11	55.0
PA	[illegible]	[illegible]	12	60.0	4	20.0	3	15.0
PH	[illegible]	[illegible]	9 10	45.0	4	20.0	3	15.0
SA	[illegible]	[illegible]	12	60.0	2	10.0	2	10.0
VO			9	60.0	4	20.0	3	15.0
SC	6	30.0	10 4	45.0	2	10.0	3	15.0
PC	6	30.0		50.0	2	10.0	2	10.0
EN	0	0.0		20.0	10	50.0	6	30.0

January

Sub-Domain Score Distribution

	0 - 25		26 - 50		51 - 75		76 - 100	
Sub-Domain	Number of Students	% of Total	Number of Students	% of Total	Number of Students	% of Total	Number of Students	% of Total
AP	0	0.0	0	0.0	3	15.8	16	84.2
CW	0	0.0	0	0.0	3	15.8	16	84.2
VS	0	0.0	0	0.0	0	0.0	19	100.0
PA	0	0.0	3	15.8	11	57.9	5	26.3
PH	0	0.0	3	15.8	11	57.9	5	26.3
SA	0	0.0	5	26.3	10	52.6	4	21.1
VO	0	0.0	3	15.8	11	57.9	5	26.3
SC	0	0.0	4	21.1	10	52.6	5	26.3
PC	0	0.0	5	26.3	12	63.2	2	10.5
EN	0	0.0	0	0.0	4	21.1	15	78.9

Literacy Classifications:

August

Scaled Score	Literacy Classification	Number of Students	% of Total
300 - 487	Early Emergent Reader	6	30.0
488 - 674	Late Emergent Reader	10	50.0
675 - 774	Transitional Reader	2	10.0
775 - 900	Probable Reader	2	10.0

January

Scaled Score	Literacy Classification	Number of Students	% of Total
300 - 487	Early Emergent Reader	0	0.0
488 - 674	Late Emergent Reader	7	36.8
675 - 774	Transitional Reader	5	26.3
775 - 900	Probable Reader	7	36.8

Yesterday, one of my academically strong and well-mannered students transferred to another school. I lost another one, damn. Her mother spoke to me and initially said that she was upset about having her daughter leave this school (my classroom) to go to another school. The parent shared why she liked my teaching style and how I was able to relate to her daughter and keep her informed of her daughters' progress. With the parent next to me, I stopped three random teachers and asked them how they felt about our school. Candidly, one teacher rolled her eyes, another mentioned how this school was not a good place. She shared with the parent some of the behaviors that she witnessed in my classroom but acknowledged that much of the behaviors were across the board, due to a lack of proper leadership schoolwide. This teacher spoke to the parent about the high turnover rate and suggested the likelihood of it being that way the following school year. The parent was able to hear from the teachers that taking her student away from this environment was the best things in order to cultivate her academic potential. The final teacher just sighed and said, "I'm ready to transfer."

The problem with a transfer is that The Cow takes it very seriously and will attempt to block it on all levels. She has been known to hold a person's paperwork to which it is ironically "lost." She has been known to further give teachers who want to transfer a difficult time within the process. Some teachers won't even try. This cow is so menacing that some teachers would risk not signing their contract (which means they would have to come back to the same school), to seek employment in another county or attempt to start anew within the same county.

Ultimately, I encouraged the parent to want the best for her child. I further stated that if wanting the best is a different environment within a different county, then so be it!

Day 48:

A little birdie gave me a warning that they are coming for me. This news comes from one of the unlikeliest of the little birdies. I doubted her, initially. I was sure that she was one of them and would be an ass kisser to maintain a position, you know with *Coachgate* and all. She proved me wrong, showing that she earned her degree, and position, the right way. She knows exactly what she is doing. I am so thankful.

Until now, I couldn't understand why the assistant principal continued to tell me to keep my head up. And on this day was no different. This time, I asked why he always says that to me. He said that he says it to everyone. Well, I had never heard that—so I questioned it. I sure did.

Then later, this little birdie comes to me and says, "Keep your head up, stand strong and be prayed up." Um, red flag! I asked her why. She told me to come talk to her later. That later was when I learned that my name is on the tips of their tongues.

I'm told that in "the meeting" it was mentioned that they were "concerned" about me. The concern centered around these new lesson plans and that I had been submitting the wrong information, or something of that nature. The assistant principal is said to have mentioned that initially my information was on the wrong document, however; he spoke to me and I immediately resubmitted them. I'm so thankful I did.

In any event, I was encouraged to write an email to them. I did.

"Greetings [Cow],

I am again requesting assistance to have a lesson modeled using the new lesson plan format. I am striving to have a clear understanding of my expectations. Recognizing that no Professional Development was given, I am specifically requesting that there be a sample grade level lesson designed and shown to me so that I can adjust my teaching accordingly. I am assuming that [your minion] would be the person to assist with this. However, if she is unavailable, I would welcome the opportunity to observe in another colleagues' classroom.

The last time I requested that a lesson be modeled—I was shown rituals and routines (which were already in place and had been acknowledged by [your minion] that they were in fact being used). Please reference the email dated November 6th, as I am still seeking clarity on the modeled lesson but also the new lesson plan format, which will help me to align my lessons with the new lesson plan template. Upon the completion of the survey checklist issued by [your minion], I am still awaiting follow-up regarding some of the small and whole group instruction, specifically aligning to an inclusion class setting.

I would like to see the grade level coaching schedule to know when we are assigned to meet (so that my planned schedule will not be interrupted with spontaneous visits as they have been in the past). I would like to have access to the activities that are provided to our grade level. Just as I am expected to have my lesson plans ready, I would like to be clear on the schedule that was shared with us in a past meeting. To my knowledge, there was an agreement to meet and various activities that were to take place—however since Tuesday, January 19, 2016, only one meeting occurred during our planning period (at which time I was in a 504 meeting)."

I blind carbon copied the regional superintendent. Check.

Day 49:

The calm after the storm is walking into the school building feeling the tension and eyes on me. If those eyes were daggers!

As I entered the building, The Cow informed me that my email had been received. I immediately went to check my email. This is what was said, "We are on the same page. In our Coaches Meeting today, you are designated to receive support. [My minion] will speak to [you] regarding key information when she meets with you tomorrow."

During the planning meeting, everything but the right things were mentioned to further push the point that my email had been received. There was so much funny business going on in there, I had to consciously maintain my composure. Normally, my eyes, my facial expression and body language will let one know that I'm not feeling their shit. Today, I had to roll with it. I took clear and precise notes. I'm arming myself for the battle.

The Cow, her minion and this 1st Grade team came together to go over whatever they were plotting and to do damage control. Do what you need to do, ma'am. I know you all are trying to play me. I continue bracing myself.

I wrote the letter. I firmly stand behind it. A meeting was called. The regional superintendent was in the building. Check.

Day 50:

Quiet on set!

After having sent a few emails, it's somewhat quiet in my neck of the woods. I know The Cow and her subordinate minions are still plotting and planning. The plan is to remain diligent in everything that I do.

Today was our day for "art on a cart". Because our art teacher didn't have a physical classroom, she put all of her materials on a cart and brought art into the classroom. This didn't provide for much teacher planning, within the classroom, especially when she needed help with classroom management. I decided that I would need to spend my planning period in the library working on some things that had been suggested. I stopped by my team members to see if we, in fact, had a meeting planned. No one knew, which was typical of how things happened within the building. I let two of the three teachers know of my whereabouts and went on about my business, to handle some business.

After lunch, I found out from my teammates that we had a planning meeting. After I raised all this hell about The Cow and her minions not meeting with me, this "instructional coach" will deny me access to a meeting. Really? I was told that someone mentioned going to get me, but this minion "instructional coach" said not it get me and that the meeting wouldn't take long. Interesting.

I whipped out my email fingers and wrote:

"Greetings,

After speaking with members on my team, I was made aware that the team along with Mrs. [minion] met during our planning period Wednesday, February 3, 2016. I just inquired on Tuesday, February 2, 2016 that we would be meeting on Mondays, Tuesdays, Thursdays and Fridays. I was not made aware of this Wednesday meeting. I spoke to team members during the start of our scheduled planning and they were unaware of any meeting. I let at least one person know I was on my way to utilize the library during this time. I'm told that one of my team members mentioned that they would come to get me however, [the minion] said "don't worry about it-this won't take long".

I am concerned as to why you all would meet without me?".

I pressed send and waited. Shortly after the email was sent, I received an email from the regional supervisor, in which she responded to all those that had been carbon copied on the email. Plain and simple, she responded, "Good question"?

Check, again!

Day 51:

Righteous rage

Because of the way things have been going, I continued to counterattack with emails—sending them to the right people (I hope). We had to do an evaluation yesterday, in lieu of a faculty meeting. We were told that we had to stay in the computer lab to complete the surveys. Oh, really now?

So, basically, you have your minions on watch, guarding these surveys with their lives and reporting back to you every little detail. Since there is no real way in which we dispose of the "CONFIDENTIAL" survey links—I wonder what you do with them? I wouldn't be surprised if those minions complete more than one survey for that cow. A mess.

I went back to my room and whipped out, yeah—you guessed it...my email fingers!

"Greetings,

Evaluations are a critical component to improvements in our educational and leadership practices, just as I am evaluated as a teacher in the privacy of my room, it is my opinion that teachers should be allowed to evaluate their leaders in privacy and not in a whole group. Yesterday's process regarding school leader's evaluation raises concerns on several levels.

Per your instruction, the certified staff met after school in the computer lab and classified staff met in the media center with the K-1 instructional support staff [i.e. the maggot] to complete the supervisor surveys. I'm striving to understand why we weren't sent a link and allowed to complete the survey in the privacy of our classrooms as opposed to having a link printed and passed out by our computer technology teacher [i.e. The Slug]. Is it customary to have a teacher (who is on my same level) be in charge of completing supervisor surveys?

I also question the method used to collect the printed links. We placed them in a box, but where do those printed survey links go and how are they disposed of? The entire process seems a bit confusing. Not to mention, the survey for the assistant principal did not work—so we weren't able to complete a survey for him. When can we expect this to be resolved?"

The Cow first responded to the entire school body.

"Awesome Staff,

Please note that [the assistant principal] and I consulted with the district yesterday about the codes they sent that were not working for his survey.

We were provided key details regarding creating new codes. [assistant principal] and I printed them, and the new codes will be available today in the lab for survey completion. [regional supervisor] requested that we build teacher capacity and allow staff members to support the process of the survey completion by the designated deadline. With that said, I indicated that PBIS team members would support the process for staff surveys. In addition, I shared that ["instructional coach"] and Teacher of the Year, could also be supportive of this process. However, due to varying obligations, all designated staff may not be available to support a process of this nature.

The Instructional surveys for Grades 3-5 were completed by [The Slug] and "Smiles," with the exception of their own. The Parent Surveys are being supported by [the parent liaison].

Again, our goal is to work collaboratively and to support all processes as outlined by [the school] and the district. Let's work together to get stronger and better in all that we do!! Thank you so kindly!"

She then she replied to me:

"Please see the email correspondence sent to all staff. I hope that the email correspondence that I sent to staff may address any concerns you have regarding surveys. If not, I will [be] happy to discuss it with you personally. Enjoy your day!"

I replied to both emails. To her I sent:

"Greetings [cow],

Thank you so much for your expeditious response. However, I am still unclear as to why we as teachers are unable to do surveys in our classroom. Please send me a copy of the law (policy or procedure) that states that we are unable to do this in our classroom.

You mentioned if I have any more questions you would be willing to speak to me personally. Per [the regional supervisor], all communication between you and I will be via email, unless it is a staff meeting or a group setting."

I further replied all, to the entire school body:

"Greetings [cow],

Thank you so much for your expeditious response. However, I am still unclear as to why we as teachers are unable to do surveys in our classroom. Please send me a copy of the law (policy or procedure) that states that we are unable to do this in our classroom.

I asked in a previous email, "Is it customary to have a teacher (who is on my same level) be in charge of completing supervisor surveys"? You did state that you have the teacher of the year assist (kudos to her); however, you still did not state whether or not this was a State of Georgia / County policy or procedure for teachers to do so. So, I am asking again. You also did not address the appropriate means of disposing the survey links. When we return the printed survey links to the designated teachers, where do they go and how are they disposed of? Please also forward me the policy and procedure as to how this should be handled. I am still confused."

By the end of the day, she did an all call over the loud speaker asking to see me in the front office. Of course, she tried to "Deebo" a conversation. I expressed that I did not want to speak to her in private, preferring to have a conversation in the presence of my team or within a meeting setting. She seemed annoyed! Who cares!!!

Day 52:

I have called out some people. I'm on your ass! Step up and do your job or STEP DOWN! And I'm not finished yet. But I will say this...people are scrambling trying to pull together paperwork to justify what they haven't been doing.

As I prepared to get out the building, to attend my own children science fair, the maggot decides she needs to see me. I give her a bit of time to see what she has for me. Of course, it's more documentation. Wanting to know what they can do to assist me. Oh, but of course.

Well, for starters, stop micromanaging me and these other adults. You can stop treating people as if we are incompetent. Don't try to handle me, as if I am one to be "handled" because you can't! Do your job and help us when we need help. Write that down!

Day 53:

"I admire you," is what a teacher walked up to me and stated today. I asked why? She said that she saw the emails from the prior week and she was glad that someone finally spoke up.

"You are wild" is what a male teacher said as I passed his classroom. He said that he finally saw the emails, which he ignored initially because he didn't have time to add more work on his plate. He said when he read the back and forth, he had to laugh.

If more teachers would speak up to the foolishness then it would no longer be about me. It may look like I am a troublemaker to some, but I'm really not. I'm just tired of the bullshit. We are better than this and we deserve better. What we are doing does not qualify as supporting our students. Supporting them becomes very difficult when you have so called leadership on your ass for stupidness.

Day 54:

We had a meeting after school today to discuss Saxon phonics. We convened in the parent liaison room to listen to a conference by phone and watch the screen as the caller spoke about something that I didn't really care about. I have no idea what's going on—can I see a sample of the materials, please? I made multiple exits to go do other things. My mind was consumed with the mailing of this letter to the board.

"My name is…I am a teacher at [the most horrible school EVER]. I write this letter and respectfully request that a thorough investigation be conducted based on the actions of our school administrator, Dr. cow. We have some great educators, who are committed to educating the children of [this failing county]. However, it is a difficult task to accomplish when your administrator is harassing, bullying and intimidating her staff. Kindly review the building turnover rate and speak with staff at the building and you will see that something is impacting our teachers and student performance.

At the beginning of the 2015-2016 school year, I was moved from one grade level to another, without any notice. When I began to ask solid questions regarding my move, I became the focus of various forms of harassment, bullying and intimidation. As I continued to stand my ground, I began to notice the many ways in which my requests for assistance and guidance from instructional coaches went unnoticed.

I have sat in meetings where I was accused of having an attitude. I have had my integrity challenged and made to feel incompetent. The paraprofessionals that work inside my classroom have come to my defense on several occasions, regarding condescending allegations brought forth to hurt me. I have written emails requesting clarity on why I was left out of a meeting, to which [regional superintendent] has even intervened, seeking the clarity as well. To my knowledge, the behavior of ostracizing me still remains unexplained and unanswered. I am left to assume that my requests of assistance, via numerous emails, made me a target-yet again. There are several staff that have experienced the same.

I am desperately asking for someone to investigate the nature of the leadership within this school. I have reached a point where I feel unstable at times, my blood pressure continues to reach unsafe levels, and this environment is not healthy. I do not wish to be anyone's target, and I made this clear at the beginning of the school year-when I was sent to internal affairs unjustly. I am asking that someone reach out to teachers, and ensure that their truths will not be retaliated against. We need help; we need real changes. We need an environment that is safe for teachers to teach so that student achievement is of the utmost importance. I am begging for someone to stop this unfair treatment, stop the harassment and bullying."

As I prepared the envelopes for my mail—I was dropped a message. What I took from this message was a simple acknowledgement that yes, I may be experiencing a dry valley however go through it to get to the mountain top. Oh, I indeed will. I felt that this was confirmation that I am righteously aligned with the right way to do things. I couldn't wait to get out that damn meeting. Straight to the post office, certified returned receipt please and thank you!

Day 55:

I sent my letters to the board yesterday. I sent one to internal affairs and carbon copied the other two to the attention of the regional superintendent and the superintendent. Although I don't have much faith in what they will do, I felt relieved that the process has started. I needed this moment.

Day 56:

I saw that my letter has been received, as of yesterday. It's on now!! I began to outline some strong bullet points in preparation for a meeting with these people.

At the end of the day, The Cow called me on the school line and told me to meet her in the parent liaison room before I left for the day. I asked what the meeting would be in reference to. She sucked her teeth and stated that I should meet with her before I left for the day. Really?

She is so sick and twisted. I will not be meeting with her. In fact, I sent her an email to let her know that I would not be meeting with her. Of course, I blind carbon copied her supervisor and also quoted the regional supervisor. I don't really have time for this Cows' foolishness. I took my time with my lesson plans and rolled out the back door. Off to relax for the weekend but also prepare for battle.

By the time I got home, there was an email awaiting me. The regional supervisor intervening? She requested my presence in a meeting. Of course I will be there! From that moment on, I prepared. I decided that I would begin my petition[1], just in case I needed to take this one step further. Of course, the thought of a petition unnerved me. It's almost like, there is no turning back. I ran for it. By 9 at night, I had called, texted and left messages for any person whom I thought would want to sign the petition. I called past and present teachers. I had some yes's, I had some no's and I had some that wanted to call their legal representation, which pretty much meant a slow no. That's fine too. There was one return phone call that took me by storm. This particular teacher was so comfortable in her new position that she was what I would call "*afraid.*" She told me in so many ways how this wouldn't work, how it's been done before, how she didn't want to lose her "sweet" position that she

[1] The petition states, "I am signing this petition acknowledging that I am aware (through witnessing or being the victim) of several forms of harassment (i.e. bullying, intimidation tactics, demeaning and demoralizing comments) by Dr. [Cow]."

currently has. While I understand all that, I don't know why it took me forever to hang up with her. I'm not begging for your signature, by far. I'm asking and if you say no-I'm fine with that as well. But for some reason, I couldn't shake this call. Even after I hung up the phone, having fought every naysaying thing thrown at me—I was defeated. I took that defeat to my bed. I laid right on top of it, I snuggled up with it and almost accepted it. When I spoke to my husband the following morning, I opened up and gave him the raw and honest pieces. I told him I was afraid and that I allowed one phone call to seal my defeat. His message to me was so powerful and so very needed. In summary, he said,

"Denmark Vessey, Harriett Tubman, Nat Turner, Ida B Wells…think about how many times they were told no, but they did it. Those who are willing to be down, whether it's 2, 3 or 4—be solid as a rock. It's going to come. Look at the five percent culture, it started with the Father. We are the few. The Black Panthers started with two, Huey and Bobby. The Black Liberation Army (BLA) started with a couple of people. Some don't end up with the right people…but look at the legacy. You have the truth, the courage and the evidence. Keep your head up. Sometimes it's lonely. You know your place in the Universe. Divine Intelligence has chosen you—whether you like it or not. It's tough to go against systems, you represent the energy of your ancestors. Your intelligence frightens her. Your ability to influence scares her. The ones you think will be there will be absent—you won't be able to find them, the ones who you think are scared might be the ones who help you. Keep doing what you know is right".

I'm ready…I'm focused again! As soon as I acknowledged that I was ready, I received a phone call that said they would sign the petition. I also received about 2 more that said they wouldn't—but I felt that I could continue. I wasn't broken. My entire day was spent going to those who said yes. I sat, conversed and strategized. My weekend centered on getting my thoughts together, being organized and focused on the monumental task.

Day 57:

The Cow didn't speak to me when I walked into the building today. GOOD!! Little does she know, we hate seeing her first thing in the morning anyway. Wait, let me speak for self. I HATE SEEING HER ASS! So, really, you don't have to speak to me. It's better that you don't.

I get to my room and I have an email at 7:30 for a meeting at 8:30. I'm so ready. I have everything and then some more. Please, believe I know what this meeting is about and I know what you are trying to do.

Basically, during the last parent teacher conference I had a parent mention that the final grade from Semester 1 didn't look correct. I agreed. We worked out the numbers and from what I could tell, it seemed the grade should be a "D." I explained to the parent that I couldn't change the grade and that she would need to speak to the assistant principal specifically, because that's who handles the online system for grades.

The parent spoke to The Cow because she didn't see the assistant principal on the date of the conference. I'm sure The Cow thought she had something on me, so she got busy. The devil is always busy. In the sick twisted way in which she works, she went and told her minion-the maggot one. The maggot was supposed to tell the assistant principal; however, he never got the message. Coincidence? I should think not.

Well, when the assistant principal received the information, the parent was irate. The parent must have felt that her strings were being pulled, yanked, tugged or whatever. So the parent came with much attitude—which was calmed by the assistant principal. The assistant principal reached out to me to get all the information I had on the student. I provided EVERYTHING!

In this meeting, I was able to defend all these accusations that were being thrown at me by The Cow. I showed proof that I sent out the appropriate documentation. I showed proof of the child's grades. I showed work samples, conference sign in sheets and conferencing documents. It was great! The Cow took plenty of notes—I just hope she put down how great I am.

So, after not being able to hem me up on this false "charge," I was summoned to the office at the end of the day, along with her maggot and the assistant principal. The Cow began with her fluff and acted as if she was going to tell me about my certification and how I needed to submit documentation to the district regarding several plans of action. After she faked that, I was presented with a Professional Development Plan (PDP). Bullshit!

You thought I would sign it? You a dummy! I told her that I would not be signing it. I didn't. I remained composed and took all of her fraudulent paperwork with me—along with a copy of the one that she wrote on stating that I "refused" to sign. Fuck you very kindly and have a nice day!

With all of the bullshit, I forgot my youngest son's birthday. Just as the recent days, I picked him up from school. I was drained. I wished him a happy birthday and my mind quickly went into overdrive. I wasn't prepared. I came home with nothing prepared to celebrate him. No cake, no ice cream, not even a special dinner. I didn't even remember to buy him a birthday card.

My husband was working out of town, so he wasn't able to pick up the slack. Not to mention, things were on the rough side for us as we both were dealing with stressful events at work and distance. There was distance of the miles, distance of the heart, distance in communication, distance in both of our minds and we were lacking the ability to reason with one another. Everything in my life was going through hell.

So here I was, alone, feeling broken, frustrated and missing our sons 10th birthday. I apologized. I was being consumed, even when I didn't want to be. Sad, frustrated, and mad at myself—I apologized. That was the best that I could do, even though it could never be enough. As lovingly as he could, he said, "It's okay, mom. I know you had a rough day." Still that was no excuse. None of this was like me. Unable to fix it or come up with a real solution, I isolated myself in my room and slept the pain away.

Day 58:

The Cow wasn't here today. Oh, how happy I am. I am unsure why she is out, but the fact that she isn't here lifts the dark cloud that hovers over this place. You would have to really be here to see the tension and then see it lifted. This thing is pure evil.

One of her minions, The Slug, was sorely sad throughout the day. She had her eyes and ears open though, ready to report back. She didn't speak to me today. Who cares? That just means you don't have to be fake today. How about a round of applause?

Throughout the day, teachers wanted to know what was going on. Of course, the news of the petition is on a lot of lips. I'm so surprised because the one teacher, who is a pillar of strength, decided that she would sign the petition. I'm really glad she is willing to move with the group versus alone. I think it's better when we can stand together and show that this is in fact this Cow's character.

I spent much of the day organizing my notes and thoughts. I printed emails that I forgot about and was able to put them with the other documents that brings to life the levels of harassment that is exhibited while in this building. It should be an interesting meeting with the regional supervisor.

The funny, but not ha-ha funny, thing about it all is that I am not sure what to expect. In one moment, I think this will help us all and then in the next moment, I know that there are teachers who have tried yet nothing has happened. I think that any acknowledgement of harassment for one will open the flood gates for not only the harassment of others but the notion that no one has done anything in all this time. It's possible that peoples' livelihoods will be in jeopardy and I know people will fight to protect all that. Just as I am fighting to protect mine, my name and my sanity. It must stop.

Day 59:

My meeting yesterday lasted from 3:30 until 7pm. It was a great meeting. Of course, they stay away from words such as "harassing,", "bullying," etc. but just know that I won't. I'm pretty smart, I won't give away all my jewels. I didn't mention the petition, that is now 16 people strong. I won't mention that. I will, however, allow you to do what you say you will do. And if you don't—we will come back unified and ready!

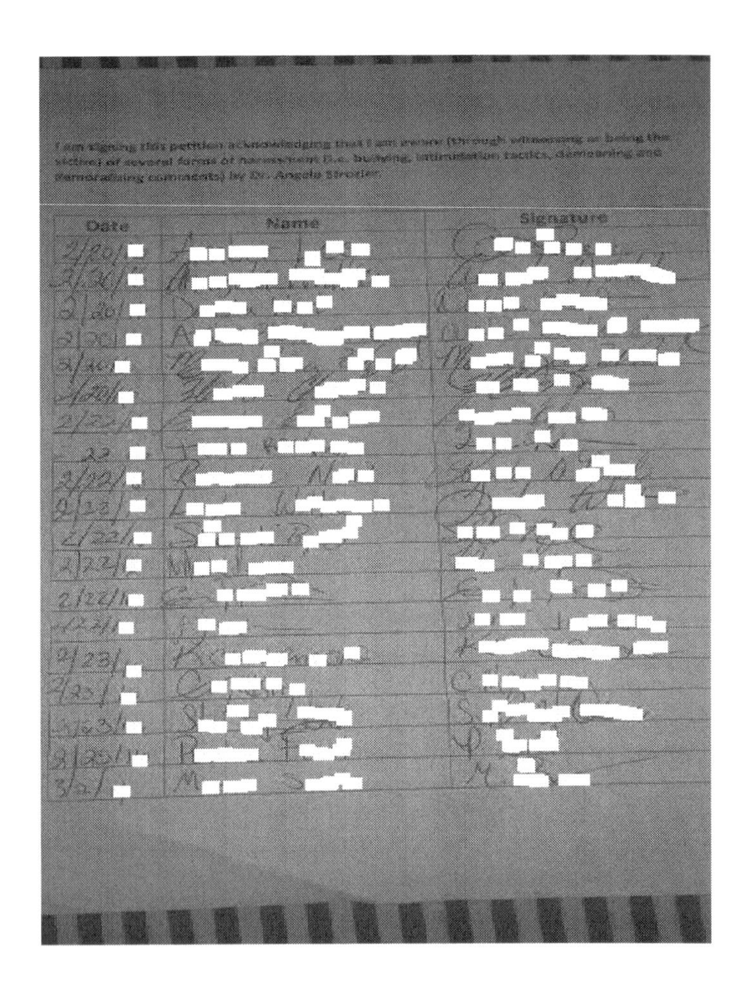

I am signing this petition acknowledging that I am aware (through witnessing or being the victim) of several forms of harassment (i.e. bullying, intimidation tactics, demeaning and demoralizing comments) by Dr. Angela Strozier

Date	Name	Signature

The school day was alright. The Cow was in full effect; however, she didn't come near me. That's a plus. I felt like I rocked out and taught some strong lessons for my students.

The afterschool meeting was ridiculous, as always. The Cow spoke for about 45 minutes on nothing in particular. Then we had a representative from an insurance agency speak at 3:45 pm. Interestingly enough, he continued on through 4p. In regular fashion, I left. To my understanding, we are only contractually obligated to stay until 4pm. After that, I feel like you in my business and lack care or concern for the things that are an utmost priority for me.

Reflecting on how I just missed my son's birthday, I knew that making more time for my family was urgent. Communications with my husband and I were suffering. At times, I felt he couldn't relate to what I was dealing with. My children, my husband, my family takes precedence over all this work-related crap, yet I was distant to everyone. They were becoming casualties of this war and I didn't quite know how to save them, nor myself.

As I went to clock out, the time system was down. I attempted to clock out anyways. I acknowledged the time that I was out because I don't want this to come back on me. I know how things operate here. The Cow mentioned that we didn't want to miss the next portion of the meeting. I, along with another teacher, stopped to acknowledge what she said. I questioned what would happen next. The Cow mentioned a vote. I asked what the vote was about. The Cow, being dismissive, never looked up and ignored my question. I giggled and walked away. She likes to play games like this. "I" don't really have the time. I don't want anything to do your foolishness.

Day 60:

When the dark clouds move to the side and the sun rays penetrate—it's such a great feeling. The Cow was absent and with every day she is away, the energy in this place is lifted. It's as if the gloom just subsides. You would really need to be in here to see it. I'm telling you, it's crazy how it happens.

Last night, I was awakened with a word for one of the minions, the maggot specifically. I must let her know, respectfully, that I do not trust her and to give her a scripture. Now, anyone who knows me knows I understand the Universal power and respect spirituality but bible study and study of the scriptures—I have long since moved away from that. However, I knew where to go to get the full scripture. I mean, you have to speak the same language in order to get an understanding—right?

So, what came to me was "We wrestle not with flesh and blood." I looked up the biblical scripture, which was Ephesians 6:12[2] and it states, "For we wrestle not against flesh and blood, but against principalities, against powers, against the rulers of the darkness of this world, against spiritual wickedness in high places."

Hmph, so befitting of this situation and these wicked, wicked people.

Day 61:

I'm so glad I have been in a good space. I have made it to work, on time, all this week. Why? Because I have been feeling like

---

[2] King James Version; Dictionary Concordance

it's my week. There's so much going on, and so many teachers are standing against the foolishness. I'm thankful.

The Cow wheeled her little cart into my room to observe me. Great! I was so on point. We covered what was in our lesson plan and a bit more. The one thing I know she will try to get me on is the fact that I was sitting when she entered. I remained sitting until I finished what I was doing. Fact is, I was sitting because my promethean board pen was missing and I had to write out everything that I needed my students to copy.

The day went successfully, without many incidents. Kind of! During my so-called meeting with my "instructional coach," I let her know what I had been thinking, feeling and what had been confirmed. I spoke to her "woman-to-woman." I let her know that I didn't trust her. I explained my reasoning, which surrounds her claiming to be a woman of God, yet she is going along with the wickedness in the building. She inquired of what wickedness and I candidly told her. I let her know that it was difficult to know whether she was trying to help me or actually sabotage me. I didn't quite know the difference. She claimed that she had no knowledge of what was going on in the building and that she was not involved, wasn't trying to get me fired.

Interesting! I never said a thing about being fired. Yet, you did. Interesting. Also, this conversation let me know that I still shouldn't try to trust her. Snakes move in a certain way that lets you know what they are about. I see her extremely clear. I'm sure she will run and tell the snake charmer, The Cow. I'll wait.

I stayed at the school to accomplish posting my lesson plans in a timely manner. I posted my lesson plans but I noticed that my lesson plan folder was missing. I recovered the folder, however there was only one lesson plan within the [possibly] deleted file. Interesting.

Interestingly enough, I was observed by The Cow today. I was on point—students learning, teacher teaching. One thing that I anticipate her documenting is my sitting down at the computer desk. That would be true. My pen for the promethean board was missing—as a result I had to work through everything from behind the computer desk, the children were engaged though! They were learning. Please document that!

Day 62: Leap year

My students turned out in their nice leap year shirts. I was so proud. Way back at the beginning of the month I sent home a letter asking parents to help their child with a leap year shirt and be as creative as they wanted to be. It turned out to be an awesome, creative project.

At some point, I began to feel really sluggish and my chest began to hurt. I figured my blood pressure was rising. I went to the nurse to get my blood pressure checked. She didn't have a blood pressure machine cuff. I went to another teacher who has similar issues. She wasn't at school. I just felt drained.

I walked from one classroom to the next, searching for a blood pressure cuff. I approached the assistant principal to inform him of my dilemma. "I don't feel well, and I really need to have my blood pressure checked".

He responded, "Did you check with the nurse?"

I shook my head "yes" and answered, "She doesn't have one."

My assistant principal looked at me puzzled and said, "How is it that the *nurse* doesn't have a blood pressure cuff? Did you check with Mrs. [so and so], she has been dealing with blood pressure related issues? She might have one."

In this quick exchange of going back and forth about who might have a blood pressure cuff and why this person doesn't have a blood pressure cuff, I saw The Cow watching us. I whispered to the assistant principal, "Here *she* comes."

The Cow butted in and stated, "I need to meet with both of you right after school."

I informed her that I had an IEP meeting scheduled right after school. She said to meet her after that. Whatever. It's quite interesting that neither of us had prior knowledge of a meeting that would take place right after school. Not an email sent, nothing planned ahead of time, no consideration for other meetings or events that occur after the children are released for the day. Just meet her afterschool.

The day progressed as they typically do. There were several classroom disruptions to the point that children had to be removed from the classroom. Since the assistant principal swiftly handled many of the behavior problems, he was the go-to person. I had to hand deliver a child to his office after the disruptions became insurmountable for three adults in room 113. The Cow saw me come out of the assistant principal's office. I'm sure she assumed that we were in cahoots when in reality we were dealing with ongoing student behaviors. From what seemed to be out of nowhere, she told me to bring my lesson plans to the afterschool meeting. Very interesting.

Because of this meeting, I am determined not to have to leave and go to the hospital. The last thing she needs to even think is that I run from things like her. Not even in my vocabulary. I face her head on. I'm so ready.

By the time I go to meet with her, she is already gone. I wonder what all this is about. It wouldn't take long for me to find out. She is inquiring about my lesson plans because the online folder has miraculously disappeared. Such a set up-but I see right through this cow. I see right through it. I have everything on my flash drive anyhow. Tomorrow should prove to be even more interesting.

Day 63:

This unintelligent animal has me all the way fucked up! How about she calls a meeting—well has the assistant principal call me over the loud speaker to ask me to meet at 2:30. No problem. Being proactive, I asked what I needed to bring. I was informed just to come to the meeting. Of course, when I strive to be on time, there is an issue with the school buses in which I must remain with the students awaiting a late bus.

I arrive to the parent room, where an RTI meeting is taking place. I wasn't sure if this is the location of where I need to be since things change so frequently around this HELLementary. The Cow, who is in this other meeting, lets me know that she planned to meet with me along with the assistant principal. We move to the assistant principals' office. The Cow tells me that we will meet on Thursday to discuss last week and this week. I excuse myself to ask what are we talking about. This serpent whispers, "your PD". I abruptly state, "oh, no, I don't even acknowledge that." I let her know that I have a letter prepared to submit because her information is incorrect.

I tell you where I messed up...I should have had my letter ready to go. I bet I have it ready on Thursday. I was so tired last night fooling around with my flash drive, ensuring that ALL my lesson plans were intact. And they were. I was just too tired to exert any more energy on the foolishness. Well, tonight, it will be complete. I have no time for this Cow and her harassment.

Today was a wacky day. I had a student swinging chairs because she was in trouble. She hit two students that were just innocent bystanders. I had another student cut up because she lost privileges. She tried to tear things off my walls and erase my board. I literally had to pick this child up and sit her on the outside of my door.

This school is highly ineffective because some of the people who are in leadership positions (specifically The Cow and her herd), like to keep children calm by allowing them to do things that reinforce the undesired behaviors. I should never see my students, or any student for that matter, in the offices playing on the computer after having such destructive behaviors. This is typical of what happens to handle disruptive behaviors. This place is ridiculous.

Parents cut up, refuse to meet with administration, and do so in front of their children...how then can we be effective? What message are you sending to your child? There is no respect for authority in this school. The climate sucks ass and it's not going to get better. The state needs to come on in and shut this hell hole all the way down.

Day 64:

I sent a follow up letter to the regional supervisor to see if there was any resolve or conclusion to our last meeting. I received a response to my letter…interesting. I was told, "As we discussed, teach your class and carry yourself as a professional. Control what you can control".

Am I the one being unprofessional? Because I refuse to be a mat for this cow? I don't understand—but then again, I do. As they say, the squeaky wheel gets the oil…well in this case I'm getting the shit that rolls downhill. I don't even know if that makes sense, but it feels like shit. And I'm tired of it.

What it basically feels like is that I won't be getting any support. Of course, I *knew* not to expect too much, however it's quite interesting that this was all she stated. Considering we spoke for three-and-a-half hours. I guess her giving me a book and allowing me to vent my frustrations, express my anger and describe the challenges we faced within one of the schools in her region was a way to shut me up for the moment. Right!

I'm just waiting on the next move. I just need to be correct in the way I move so that others won't be affected negatively. I already know I will be blackballed. It just comes with the territory and the nature of their game.

After work, I went to the county office to see if I could file a grievance and get information on the guidelines for a PDP. I spoke to someone in personnel and was told that there was no policy on the PDP and that the principal could write them based on what they deem inappropriate or something needing a remedy. Bullshit? That doesn't even sound right. Well, I can't expect the "enemy" to hand over that information—now can I?

So I was sent to the office of Internal Affairs to get information on the grievance. That proved to be ever so helpful—not at all. I was told to write down the name of my school on some sticky note. I already felt this was a set up. The information that was passed to me, was that I would have to file a grievance with the area supervisor. It sounds like I have to go back through the regional superintendent—who is not a help. But let's see.

I proceed to the next office and let the head of security (who was quite pleasant, by the way) know what I needed to do. There is about an hour before the offices close, so I am expecting to get in and get out. I'm thinking I will get the grievance paperwork, look it over, and submit it in a day or so. No sweat. I find a comfortable seat in the lobby and wait.

As the offices are closing, the head security apologies and suggests that I write my name on yet another post it note where he can see if anyone can speak to me. I'm fine with this—I think. He returns to tell me that someone will be out shortly.

As the life of a teacher would have it, the area supervisor/regional superintendent appears and looks rather annoyed. She has her secretary in tow. She greets me with, "What's going on?" Not so much in an I care about what's going on but with a "What the fuck do you want now," sort of connotation. So, I explained to her that I wanted to get (or file) a grievance. She asked me why. I told her that I felt that I am still being harassed.

The regional supervisor brought up every thought except the grievance. She mentioned that we spoke for over three hours, she asked me if I spoke to the principal or took any of her suggestions. I explained that those issues hadn't resurfaced and I didn't feel comfortable bringing it up at that time and would discuss it when the opportunity presented itself. I further told her that I came to the office, not to see her, but to get a grievance and to ask about a policy concerning the PDP that the principal put me on for attendance.

Oh, how annoyed and upset we became. I was accused of being manipulative, insubordinate and was told many times that I cannot tell her (the regional supervisor) how to do her job. I asked for clarity on how she thought that I was attempting to tell her how to do her job. She mentioned my email.

This email: "I would like to follow-up on the meeting we had on Tuesday, February 23rd. I know that you are really busy but I am feeling more and more uncomfortable each day that I have to endure the pressures of this increasingly unsafe and hostile environment."

Might I remind you that I sent this a week after our three-hour meeting. I wasn't rude—just inquisitive. I'm not sure how this translated to being manipulative or even attempting to tell someone how to do their job. But okay!

To be completely honest, this whole conversation was out of line. It took place in the lobby and it escalated to the point where this lady, the regional superintendent was yelling at me. And for what? I had to remain poised because I was already accused of being insubordinate and manipulative. I was so frustrated that I had to endure the humiliation. Yes, I was completely humiliated. I was frustrated and there was nothing I could do, that would remove me from an unfavorable light. I wanted to curse her ass out, but then this would validate the insubordination claim. I wanted to get up and walk away from the bullshit, but again I risk being looked at as insubordinate. I had to endure—and it wasn't pretty.

I actually cried. Not because I was nervous or scared—I cried because I felt I had no option, no support and I couldn't say a thing to truly defend myself. So the whole situation just validated, for me, that help will not be coming from these once upon a time educators. It's all for self, at this point. But I already knew that-didn't I?

That night, I showered with my husband while he just held me. He allowed me to be vulnerable. I hadn't been able to let my defenses down for quite some time. I allowed the warmth of the shower to rinse the deep-rooted tears that poured from my soul. I cried heavy tears. I was tense and my body was in a constant state of knots. I was angry and my heart was often hard and calloused. I was frustrated and unclear of what the next step should be. I didn't want to be insubordinate or manipulative. I couldn't wrap my mind around whether I was doing the right thing or whether I was in the wrong. I was hateful and I didn't have anything kind to say to The Cow nor could I wish her well. I was disgusted that I could be pushed to this point. It seemed as if I were at a point of no return. I was frightened. I wasn't sure if I was doing too much or not enough. What would happen if I kept pushing? How would this end?

I let it all release through tears that had been welled up in my soul. I cried tears that I didn't know I had. My husband held me up without saying a word. In this moment, I felt like giving up. He must have felt my emotions because he said, "What do you want to do? Do you want to keep going or do you want to stop?"

Through my tears, I said, "I don't know yet." He washed my body. We bathed in silence. As the suds rolled from my body, mixed with the warm water and my hot seething tears, I knew that I had to continue. I had come too far to just give up. My rage was righteous. My feelings were real. What I experienced was not some figment of my imagination. Unfortunately, it was real. It was happening. Not only to me, but it happened to other teachers in the past and was happening again this year. The Cow had been accustomed to harassing and bullying teachers. Each year, each time, she would win. She would get away with causing destruction, mental manipulation through stress and fear while the county offices allowed it. Through negligence, they allowed her to be a bully while pretending not to notice.

By the time the water stopped dripping from the showerhead, I looked at my husband and said, "I'm not ready to stop."

Day 65:

Today was all around horrible. I mean, it was alright that The Cow was out to pasture somewhere but the students cut up something serious. Evil eyes threw a chair at one of the paraprofessionals in my room. I had to have all the children evacuated and go into the hallway until things could be handled.

Then when the mother came, after the assistant principal called her—she refused to communicate with the assistant principal. Thankfully, I have a pretty good relationship with this parent-but it's not enough. She blatantly ignored the assistant principal in front of the child. I mean completely disregarded him. She took her child and walked out the school. So rude! And if we acted like this—then what?

This school is hell. We don't have support from the supervisor of this building. While she is so busy destroying the morale, and beating up on her staff, the school continues to fail. A lot of the children are not on grade level and we (teachers) are doing our best to stomach this hostile environment. We are under attack from all perimeters. At war with the supervisor of this building, in a battle with the children and confronted daily with the lack of proper parenting by busy parents. It's a mess!

Oh, guess what? My online gradebook is messed up…could this be someone fucking with me again? Probably—but I have no proof yet. It never ends.

Day 66:

Again, The Cow wasn't here. You have to be here to understand the happiness one feels when she is out. That dark cloud is lifted and the sun can shine. Sometimes the sunshine isn't appreciated until it's missed or not visible often. I'm so sick of dark clouds. I'm sick of this place.

By the end of the day, a parent comes looking for paperwork that was supposed to be given to her during the impromptu setup meeting orchestrated by The Cow. I escorted her to the counselor to figure out whether there was any additional paperwork the parent needed. The counselor called The Cow on her cell phone. The call is on speaker phone. The parent asks the necessary questions and of course The Cow curtails the questions, brings me into the situation as if I failed to provide the parent with the documentation. Um, no!

So, basically, they dropped the ball-yet again. She attempted to throw me under the bus in the process, more than once. It's no longer in my court, as I have done exactly what I needed to do. When children are given important documents to go home, I email the parents and text them so that they know to look out for it. This one, buddy, isn't on me! I know you tried it.

Day 67:

I received an early morning word from someone (Psalms 37: 4-9). Although I am not a Christian, I can accept the prayers of those who are righteously pulling for me. I know the creator—so any great energy that a person directs or asks to be directed in my path—trust I appreciate it.

During extracurricular time, the Spawn of Satan squirts hand sanitizer in a student's eye. The victim, who really isn't an innocent victim, was sent to the nurse. The parent was upset and on their way to school. Great! I need a conference with you anyway.

When the parent arrived, guess who escorted the parent down? You guessed it—the amazing super Cow! No, you aren't about to get me caught up in any drama—because I wasn't there. In fact, I was in an RTI meeting for another one of these students that y'all just keep passing along. This situation didn't happen on my watch, ma'am. Try again.

The father, barely able to comprehend, suggested that his son isn't allowed to go to the bathroom and this is why he comes home each day with stains in his underwear.

"My son tell me that you don't let him go to the bathroom," the father expresses in front of The Cow.

I'm a bit confused since this is the first time I've heard this. Not to mention it's a lie. I politely say, "Excuse me?"

As The Cow keys in to the conversation, the father repeats his statement, "My son tell me that you don't let him go to the bathroom. He come home with poop in his clothes."

Wait, what? No, his son isn't allowed to go to the bathroom alone because he plays in the restroom. I responded, "I don't know anything about his clothes being soiled, but he has plenty of opportunities to go to the restroom. In fact, he is often escorted to the restroom, by an adult, because he plays in the restroom."

The father begins to get loud and irate, "No, my son don't play in the bathroom. You don't let him go to the bathroom!"

Since The Cow isn't fit for standing up to parents or equipped to defend her teachers in a situation that is clearly not factual, I bluntly respond. "Look, your son is allowed to go to the restroom. Alone, no! With supervision, yes! I have sent you numerous emails and ClassDojo[3] messages asking you to talk to him

[3] ClassDojo is a communication app for the classroom. It connects teachers, parents and students who use it to share photos, videos and messages through the day. They use ClassDojo to work together as a team, share in the classroom

about playing in the restroom. I have not heard a response from you. I have asked you to come in and speak to me about his inappropriate behaviors. I have not heard from you. I have asked you to come in to speak about his academics and him not returning any homework. I have not heard from you. So, to say that I am the reason his clothes are not clean when he gets home is not true. Is it possible that he doesn't know how to properly wipe himself?"

The Cow just stands there looking dumb. She should know, by now, that documentation rules my life. I back up all my communications to and from parents through emails, ClassDojo and copies of anything that I send home. I'm not new to this. I am a very thorough individual. I know my shit! The child in question isn't allowed to go to the bathroom when it appears that he is avoiding classwork; which he does when he says he cannot find a pencil or needs a sharpened pencil, despite having 10 perfectly usable pencils hidden in his desk. This child goes to the restroom at our scheduled break times, however he has to go in before the other students because he cannot handle being in the restroom with anyone else.

---

experience, and bring big ideas to life in their classrooms and homes. (https://www.classdojo.com/about/)

This child also is escorted to the restroom, by an adult, during unscheduled restroom breaks so that he doesn't spend unnecessary time in the restroom. Your son, *sir*, hasn't exactly been the upstanding child you are trying to paint him as. Please, try again!

The parent moves beyond the restroom conversation and asks about the Spawn of Satan "putting" hand sanitizer in his son's eyes. "Why did you let someone put hand sanitizer in his eye?"

Annoyed that he (or anyone else) would think that I would allow someone to put hand sanitizer in another person's eye, especially children, I respond, "I didn't *let* anyone put anything in anyone's eye. I don't have any information about the incident because I was not there. It did not happen in my classroom. It happened in the gym."

After explaining these things to the parent and The Cow seeing as though there isn't anything she can add to her falsified documents against me—she quiets her "mooing" and shuffles her carcass back to her dungeon. I know she won't stop, but then again neither will I. So, I will do my best to remain righteous through this process and continue to prove them wrong.

Day 68:

Well, since they dropped the ball, yet again….an "emergency meeting" is called to appease this one parent. Basically, why are you holding the Parental Consent to Evaluate (PCE) hostage? This lady knows the process better than some of the folks sitting in the meeting. What are we doing?

Really, it's what you all get for having too many unnecessary hands in the pot. Who makes gumbo like that? Some of these wannabe chefs need to fall back and just wait until dinner is served. But no, you want to be greedy. I get it—that's why you are a cow and lack real discipline. I see it in your midsection, I so understand.

So as we scramble to ensure that all documents are together—we see that there won't be a meeting because the Lead Teacher for Special Education (LTSE) won't be available for the meeting. Wait, who called this emergency ass meeting in the first place? Y'all are doing THE most. In your attempts to fuck me over, you really are showing how unprofessional and unprepared you are. Go out to pasture. Please!

On another note, how about The Cow introduced some foolishness that they attempted to use last year-without explanation then and none now. Last year, she just started handing out school "bucks" and called them "Star Bucks." Cute. However, she didn't explain the criteria of why we were receiving them. There was no explanation how long this "game" would last. Seriously, what are we getting coupons for? I recall my class earning a coupon. I was on time picking up my children from the cafeteria. Wooop dee doo, I earned a coupon. Wow! Then my next-door classroom neighbor was on time, the same day and she earned none. So, really what was the coupon for? How do we earn them? Once we earn them, then what happens? I still have the other coupon from the previous school year! Nice try. Not!

So I'm hearing on the loud speaker that this "process" is back in full effect. I just laugh at this place. I am learning to laugh to keep from crying. If this is how you are implementing the Positive Behavioral Interventions and Supports[4] (PBIS) process, then you are sadly mistaken. Just like with all the other things that happen in this building, there are very few directives given, very little comprehensive trainings, just a lot of paperwork that makes one appear to think that we are doing something effectively. It's not working!

She can't care about this school or these children. When she allows it to go to hell like this, she can't care. This isn't the first year this school has been down in the dumps. Then to half ass with something that can work for this environment, that's not care nor is it concern. But I guess when you sit in your fancy ass chair, in a quiet office—googling shit that you want to impose on us—it doesn't really concern you. You aren't in the trenches, on the battlefield. No, you sit in the oval office consulting with people that

---

[4] "This language comes directly from the 1997 reauthorization of the Individuals with Disabilities Act (IDEA)...PBIS is based on the principles of applied behavior analysis and the prevention approach and values of positive behavior support. PBIS is a framework or approach for assisting school personnel in adopting and organizing evidence-based behavioral interventions into an integrated continuum that enhances academic and social behavior outcomes for all students. PBIS is a prevention-oriented way for school personnel to a) organize evidence-based practices, b) improve their implementation of those practices, and c) maximize academic and social behavior outcomes for students. PBIS supports the success of all students." (https://www.pbis.org/school/swpbis-for-beginners/pbis-faqs)

you have put in position so that you are not questioned but acquiesced with.

Day 69:

Certain people were out of the building today for the PBIS training. I'm still trying to figure out why many of them even attend these trainings when they clearly have expressed interests in not being here next school year. Then again, who knows. There is no real rhyme or reason to this horse and pony show. Just smile and wave.

Like most days, the children were off the hook. How can one teach in this environment? How are we even expected to? I sit and look around my classroom and they lack true motivation. Well, some of them. I have tried a number of things to help bring back or create a motivation for learning. I have students who are complacent, even at this age, about their progress. Something is wrong.

Today was a day where we attempted to learn a few things—some acted as if the information was new/foreign to them. There were too many saying, "I don't know how to do this" and "Can you help me?" A few simply checked out and started causing chaos within the classroom. I had a student say, "Why do I need to know this?" Wait a minute! You really need to know this because it's going to be the foundation for everything else you will learn.

I just had to shake my head and attempt to re-teach. I even invited a kindergartener to my 1st Grade classroom to read to my students. The student was confident and unafraid of sitting in front of wide eyes to read his story. As he read, he showed the pictures to the class and made eye contact too. I was floored.

After the student returned to his classroom, I asked my students, "What did you like about the book?" Some of the responses I heard, "I liked the book," "I liked the people," and "I liked the pictures."

I asked my students, "Do you think you could read a story to someone you didn't know well?" Most of the students quickly responded, "No." I did hear a couple of students say, "Yes," but the overwhelming no's reminded me that some of my students didn't have a lot of confidence in themselves and their own abilities. We returned to our desks to continue our studies. They were impressed by the kindergarten reading to them, but not enough to pick up their own books and read. I'm not sure how to motivate them anymore. I'm not even sure how to motivate myself at this point. I'm pretty much counting the days down. When is Spring Break again? Hurry! Please!

Day 70:

I met with an attorney last night. It was very beneficial and enlightening. My takeaways from meeting with [the attorney]:

1. Email The Cow: "Please advise me of the time, location and what's needed for the meeting on Friday, March 11, 2016. What do I need to bring to ensure that I am progressing with the documented information on the PDP? Who will be in attendance of this meeting?" During this meeting, provide a copy of the documents and letter that support my absences. Write on the top of each document, "hand delivered to [Principal] on *date*."

2. Get a copy of the employee handbook with any additional amendments and supplements.
3. Get my employee file to make sure that there aren't any surprises.
4. Send a certified return receipt letter to the board (the people who received the original letter). Amend the letter in one or two paragraphs. Mention, "I was recently apprised of my PDP. Here is documentation for the attendance in question." I do not have to reference the previous sent letter-but I should make note that this is an amendment to the original letter. Provide documentation of the absences. I can send the same information that I will provide to [The Cow].
5. Check to see if there is a teacher hotline number for complaints.

It is also noted that a PDP is discretionary. The Cow may be attempting to stack my file so it's important to pay attention to what's in the file.

It should also be noted that Georgia is a "*Right To Work*" state which means they can hire/fire for any reason. I cannot, legally, obtain an attorney until I have exhausted my administrative remedies because that could be grounds for termination. Administrative remedies for this situation would be contacting the board/chain of command (regional superintendent/area supervisor), the superintendent. I have to allow them time to respond or attempt to resolve the situation. Since no time frame was given, I have to be patient and wait. After this, the next chain of command is state agencies and then federal. All of these entities take time. The issue that I may run into, since its March (49 days left of school), time may run out before all these time restrictions run out.

I am advised to be STELLAR. I should do everything I can to have all of my affairs in order so that nothing can be added to my file without question. I also have to find out "What are mutable characteristics?" From what I looked into and understood, an immutable characteristic would be "any sort of physical attribute which is perceived as being unchangeable, entrenched and innate."

Therefore, a mutable characteristic would be something that can be changed.

I had a parent teacher conference this morning. It went well. What I found out from the parents, is that someone is coming for me. The parents were told by someone in the front office that if they had an issue with me, they were encouraged to write a grievance. The parents mentioned that they told this person that they were only here for a conference and wanted to work with me to improve their child's classroom behaviors.

We had a really good conference. It's really quite interesting that The Cow showed up at the end of the conference. She came snooping around as if invited. But we wrapped up as if she wasn't even there. Bye, Cow!

After sending my email message, our scheduled conference for tomorrow was moved up to today. I was prepared. I was asked if there were any concerns—to which I mentioned classroom behaviors. I noted that my students' behaviors seemed to improve when I used the counseling program that the school counselor suggested. I noticed, too, that when the schedule was changed (moving reading from the morning schedule and replacing it with math) my behaviors got worse. I mentioned that I used the reading block to go over social skills with the students and read to them the suggested books that the counseling model recommended. I also noted that my write ups increased and looking at the times, I was writing children up first thing in the morning.

I have children that come in angry and upset. I have children that seem to be on edge all the time. I used the morning meetings to soothe them, calm them down and teach them. We talked, we reviewed our rituals and routines. We did a lot on that carpet and to have that taken from us—I noticed a change that affected the entire classroom.

I had mentioned, a week ago, that the reason I felt this was happening was due to not using the strategies I had been using. I knew that math, first thing in the morning, wouldn't allow me to do the program because I couldn't justify being off schedule. In our reading block, I could use the program and the students would be doing something pertaining to reading, whether it's me reading to them or them reading to me.

So, The Cow allowed me to change my schedule to see if this will work for me. She also mentioned that I cannot take the children from their specials (which I used as a disciplinary action), but I could begin to take them outside as an incentive. The students can eat outside and then play for a few moments. Since this isn't "recess" but lunchtime I could get away with it. Of course, she makes it appear as if she is trying to help me—but I know the truth in this matter. She is documentation princess so all of this will be used against me shall I fail. I don't plan to fail. I won't fail!

Day 71:

(Teachers workday)

I had anticipated going to a professional development, but it didn't quite work out. I made it to work and just got to work doing the things I needed to do to catch up. I went to meaningless meetings. Well, maybe this meeting wasn't meaningless—but it reminded me that we have to be creative in our endeavors. Teaching is so temporary.

The one meaningless meeting that I did attend was with the maggot, who lacks very much knowledge. I swear she tries to fast talk to keep one from knowing that she knows shit. The point of the matter is she sits in these meetings going over the same shit, but she isn't really saying a thing. I had to excuse myself and go do some real work. I found out later she never figured out the one thing she attempted to explain to us. Sad!

The day went well. My husband brought me a yummy lunch and we were able to eat it together. It felt good.

Day 72:

So, we changed our classroom schedule and I explained to the children we would go back to our original morning meetings. They were excited. We reviewed our classroom rules, our carpet rules and some of the new incentives. The children were excited. I must admit—so, too, am I.

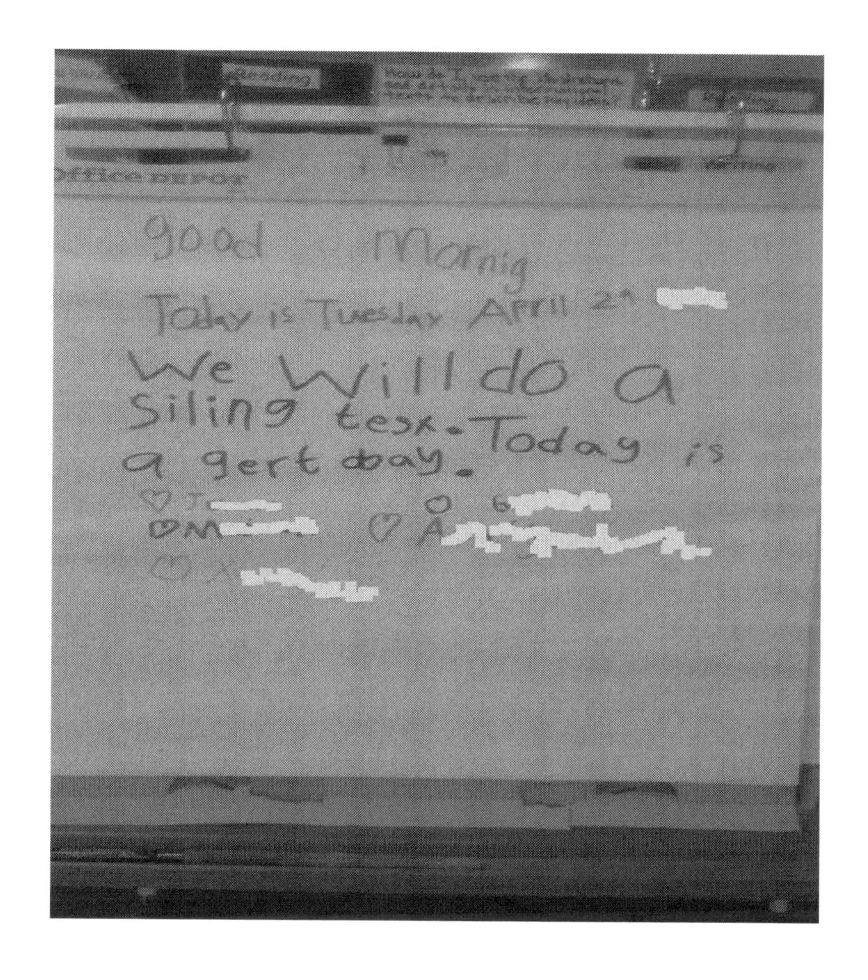

Having reading time as the students arrived in the morning allowed me to connect with my students on a deeper level. As the students arrived, we would meet one another on the carpet, and social skills training began. Well aware that many of my students missed out on social skills learning in the previous year, it was important that they gained them now. The students that missed out on their morning nurturing from their parents had an opportunity to receive it on the carpet.

With several variations of eyes on the carpet, bright eyes, sleepy eyes, hungry eyes, eager eyes, deprived eyes and even abused eyes, they were all on me. Beginning the morning with a loving note helped set the tone, even if it were only for a few minutes. Within the first few minutes of class, they heard me tell them that they were loved. They were encouraged and sometimes challenged to work through whatever they entered the classroom with. On our carpet, we reviewed our rules and practiced adding new social skills such as how to sit quietly and respectfully await their turn. We practiced sharing, caring, reading and writing. On our carpet, we enacted social skills skits and we laughed with one another. Our time on the carpet was very important to us all, as it helped curb the onset of disruptive behaviors that started long before they entered the school building.

Today was an overload of encouragement, praise and organic animal crackers for great behaviors. We ate lunch outside and the smiles were so wide. This is the class I love to see. They looked happy. I felt happy. No, today wasn't perfect, but it was far from the chaos and frustration of the past weeks. I felt like I rocked out. I felt like a teacher. I was actually able to teach a few things.

As I walked out the building, I received a phone call for an interview in another county. EXCITED!!! Indeed. I'm going to be there, wearing bells and I plan to secure this job.

Day 73:

Showing versus telling is often a different thing when it comes to those who disbelieve-so I had several students that remained inside during lunch. But the thing that pissed me off is that I have students that are leaving the cafeteria and cannot be found at some point. How is it that my students are missing? Not one or two students, but seven students missing? I'm dumbfounded. Of course, you know I think this is a set-up. Will this come back to bite me in the ass? I need to figure this out, cover my ass because this incentive is working for my students. So far-anyways!

I had a student from Georgia State visit the school and observe my class. His eyes were shocked at some of the behaviors and some of the work samples shown. Well, sir, you aren't on the North side. Truth be told, this is a better day than just last week. So I will take it. It's amazing what people think it should be but then when you show them what you have, its unfathomable. Yea, this isn't Gwinnett county-it's a struggle over on this side. And it seems that some don't care…sadly, we are the ones cast to the wayside. Students and teachers, alike.

We had a pretty good day despite those who tried it. It was a good day. I asked parents, yesterday, to begin sending in towels so that we can sit on the ground and eat our lunch. Right now, we have park benches out in the courtyard area of the school. They aren't the nicest, but they have served a great purpose. Maybe one day we can clean them up and make them look nicer.

Day 74:

Of course, some student would want to buck the process. However, I didn't leave work with a headache. The incentives are increasing. Last night I bought bouncy balls, bubbles and brought in some jump ropes. We are serious about these learn and play days. They are trying hard to do great so that they can go outside. I am so proud.

Within the public schools, that I've taught in, recess isn't built into the curriculum. Actually, recess cannot be called recess. The students are expected to release their need to move, jump, scream and simply be children, in the process of another structured "specials" class. It's quite confusing as an adult. Consider how it feels and is rationalized to a child. My class needs to move. My students need to be active and release all that jittery energy that is built through the day.

With our learn and play days, we eat lunch outside together. I enjoy being outside with the students and they enjoy it as well. I admit, its unhealthy for them to eat so fast, yet they really want to use their time to run, jump and just be. The thought of them using the new toys that they earned for outside play makes them work a little bit harder. Today, they earned the right to play with them and I look forward to gifting them with the new toys.

Even while we are outside, we are learning social skills. They talk quietly while they eat and clean up around themselves before they can go play. Usually two students volunteer to take the large trash to the custodians in the cafeteria, which means they are taking more responsibility for their role within the classroom family. Not every classmate has been able to submit to the order and direction of what we are striving to do. It's unfortunate but a consequence is a consequence. It seems that the consequence digs deeper when those who showed proper social skills are eager to share with the one or two who missed out due to their lack of proper social skills.

We had a meeting afterschool, you know, those Wednesday meetings. I actually learned a little bit. I think the teacher and assistant principal that led the meeting did a great job. Yea, it's a lot of work to do and more shit on my plate but they pulled the information off well.

At some point in the day, I began to pack up some of my things. I plan to leave a lot of stuff, but the things I want to keep I need to begin taking home. My goal is to have things out this building by Spring Break. I'm not trying to have a car full of things on the last day of school. No way! So as I am walking out the building and passing one of the rooms that The Cow hides in, she calls out my name. I walk backwards to reach the door. She asks me if the meeting is over. I told her that it was wrapping up.

Now, what do you think that was all about? I know! She saw me with an arm full of stuff. She probably wanted to see if I was stealing or else just see what I was doing. I'm laughing inside because she has rarely called me to ask me anything and since all the bull…she barely parts her lips. I ain't playing with you. Nosey ass! Stop stalking my moves.

Day 75:

We had a meeting after school, as Spring Break is upon us. She loves to call impromptu meetings. I guess she thinks she will ruin my break or my weekends. Not hardly. Well the assistant principal was out of the building and some of the leadership team that I respect was out as well. As The Cow attempted to begin the meeting, I requested someone from leadership be in the meeting. My fake "instructional coach" messed up when she asked if I would like the school counselor to be in the meeting. Oh, but of course. Because I know the school counselor is going to speak truth and light, whether The Cow likes it or not.

As with every meeting of this magnitude, I am put on the block. This time it was because I was asked, by The Cow, if everything was alright with instructional planning. I admitted that it was not good. I mentioned that the meetings were sporadic, redundant and seemed as if they were in place only to fulfill a portion of documentation.

Maybe my delivery is hard to digest but it is what it is. Don't ask me if you don't want to know the truth of the matter. So, the maggot says to The Cow, "I won't speak unless you want me to." What kind of shenanigans is this? She is trying so hard to be approved. Well, ma'am, step your certification and qualifications up and you won't have to kiss ass to keep a position. Can't I be honest?

So as the maggot begins to speak she states that she likes how I am bringing this to the attention of the "supervisor" trying to get her in trouble. Yea, I am paraphrasing but it was as if she was calling me a snitch. Oh, but wait, hold up. So I told her, just as I told The Cow, "I have mentioned this to you on several occasions." I reminded her that I was asked about how things were going and they aren't going great. Trust me, this is not the first time this has been heard. So, we go back and forth and I show how she has gone back on much of everything she has told me she would do to assist me.

Please remember, these are the same cowardly women who like to call a meeting as soon as I bring to their attention how they are not supporting me with this class. So I made mention of the fact that I was videotaped giving a lesson and was told that she would teach a lesson and allow me to videotape it. I was also told that a schedule would be created so that we both could document where we are in the meeting and the progress that's being made. I also noted that these things have yet to happen. Why else would there be a need to document our progress? I will let it marinate in their itty bitty minds for a moment.

As the "meeting" progressed, the school counselor was threatened to be kicked out of the meeting. The school counselor pointed out some flawed views and ways they were doing things. As a result, her presence was threatened. According to The Cow, "You are only here to listen. If you say something else—I will kick you out the meeting." Actually, you can't do that or else the meeting will be over. Someone should be present on the leadership team because you, Cow, cannot be trusted. Things were heated because the school counselor came to the aid of truth, as if truth needs assistance. They are a class act, The Cow and the Maggot.

As the "meeting" concluded, I asked to see the notes that were being written. That was what the regional superintendent suggested. We were to sign off in agreement of each other's meeting notes. My request was denied, citing "scribbling" and time needed to type it up in email format. I reminded The Cow that this was not what we were recommended to do. Let's go back a couple meetings. We were instructed to sign off on each other's notes and provide a copy to one another, being transparent. On at least one occasion, we had managed to accomplish this suggestion. Now today, possibly because of the way things transpired, there was no desire to share her notes. I ensured that I mentioned that she was not following the instructions of her own supervisor. What? I was only being honest! She was heated. Needless to say, I didn't get my hands on those notes. I will wait to see what the email states. I will be ready!

Day 76:

Spring break came and went by so fast! I felt refreshed, just by the nature of having some down time. Then the closer I crept to this school, the more I became upset and tired. All over again. I can't even say it's a "welcome back" kind of thing. Its agony on top of pain. I guess we do have to come back in order to continue counting these days down. But it sure is painful.

Then the maggot had the audacity to smile and speak to me. Chile' please. I just looked at her out the corner of my eye and kept walking. Maybe she thought I didn't hear her, because she came back later and attempted a hello. No, I heard you. I just chose to look beyond you. I'm sure she will "run and tell dat." That's her thing.

She is such an underling. I notice that she looks to have gained some weight. This break didn't seem to be too kind to her at all. She looks as if she has been hanging with The Cow a bit too much. A heifer, following around her counterpart. Sad!

Day 77:

Another day to strike off. We are still counting down the days until summer break. I cannot wait to get out of this place. That spring break was just a tease. It felt so good but the reality of coming back into this…UGH!

The children have been pretty good. I think they are excited to be back. The Cow hasn't started up, as far as I know. So, that's a welcome change. I have been focused on the students and trying to teach them as much as I can in the school day.

The school counselor sent out a schoolwide email yesterday about National assistant principal week, thanking the assistant principal for the contributions to the school. In indignant form, The Cow followed with an email saying thank you and that he was already acknowledged during boss's week. Really? I don't recall this. But this seems to be her theme. She does not like to recognize the contributions of others. She will go to extreme lengths to shoot someone down rather than utter a word of praise. She did this to a REAL data coach after someone acknowledged her first. She also did this to a teacher when a teacher was recognized from another teacher. So miserable she is.

This gesture of hers rubbed a lot of people wrong. One of our highly-qualified teachers put together a celebration for our assistant principal. She made bow tie trinkets on card stock and passed them out to each teacher. We were asked to write something special to the assistant principal. I thought it would be a good idea to make a large shirt out of butcher paper. I added some buttons, cuff links and a large bow tie. We presented it by placing it on the wall outside his office door. It was awesome.

With this, we already knew that we were starting a fire and war would be waged. Bring it!!!

Day 78:

Oh, the hate is real!! I heard that the maggot was quoted as saying, "If we do this for him, we should also acknowledge [The Cow]." Is she mad? Then she was also noted as saying in a meeting, "[The Cow] ain't gonna have that. Y'all spending time making bow ties when y'all should be planning." Interesting.

Just as I heard that, I saw her going into the office of the assistant principal asking for a bow tie. Seriously? You are so fake. As he was putting on her bow tie, she spoke to me. I just looked at her in her face. No words given. None! I have nothing for you. So, maggot-thing, you can think that your speaking is you taking the high road or being a bigger person. Please continue to think that. But let's not get it twisted—I told you I don't trust you and you have given me more reasons to validate my reasons. We don't have to speak. Well, you can but please know that I will continue to look you in your face and move forward. We (meaning I) will not be fake.

The dessert table was set up nicely. The children looked so amazing with their paper bow ties. The staff rocked out with their various versions of the assistant principal's bow tie fashion. Too bad he couldn't really partake of any of it due to being in a meeting with The Cow from early morning through the staff lunch hours. Oh, misery wants company—so bad! It makes no sense how she is so hateful and mean. I guess that's why her health is failing and her knees are bad from all the heavy weight she is carrying. Maybe she should get her life right.

In the meantime, we will continue to celebrate the true leader of this school throughout the entire week. Friday is walking taco day! We are bringing items to make tacos and we will continue to celebrate him despite her wickedness. Oh, and we aren't finished yet. Nope! Not yet.

Day 79:

That thang mad!! How about she sent out a long email, late into the night, talking about "It is important to know that we must all contribute to a positive school climate. However, my goal is to ensure that everyone is always included and supported in a positive manner. It is important that at no time should any staff member not feel they can participate in events that celebrate the hard work we are committed to at [this school] or to focus on the personal events outlined in the bylaws of the Sunshine Committee."

Oh, there is more…but allow me to interject my candid thoughts on this bullshit! So basically, you are mad because someone felt excluded based on the fact that they have poor social skills and poor sportsmanship when dealing with the team. Or is it that you are mad because we decided to recognize someone despite your evil attempts to thwart it? Either way, you are one miserable, unfortunate soul. I digress.

She continues, "However, I must convey that many faculty and staff brought it to my attention that they were not aware of the event for National assistant principal's Day. We must be diligent to be inclusive and inspire others from a positive perspective. At no time do we want to present events in a manner that becomes divisive as it relates to celebrating others. Please know that you must engage positively by using our Standard Procedures of Operations (SOP's) at all times to ensure a positive school climate."

This cow knows all about divisive, as she continues to do things to ostracize the faculty and staff. She has even gone so far as to tell new teachers to be loyal to her or to stay away from certain people. I have even heard staff mention that she has made comments about the current staff, in the new hires interview. How messy and divisive is this?

She further states, "All teacher activities will be conducted through the Sunshine Committee. No teacher functions will be planned without the guidance and directions of the Sunshine Chairperson or without the approval of administration. This will allow us to establish a target date for planned events while boosting staff morale, improving staff recognition opportunities, and to just enjoy interacting at work. Planning such scheduled events each month would eliminate creating isolated dates that have not been approved through administration. *All staff members that choose to operate and plan unscheduled activities without the guidance of the Sunshine Committee will be subject to the protocol for failure to comply.*"

What morale? The morale in this place is so low that its non-existent. So now she wants to quote the "Standard Procedures of Operations" surrounding the opportunity to support or recognize staff members. Really, she is mad that she didn't know what was going on, nor was she included because no one likes her ass. But did she just change work "guidelines" to accommodate her insanity? People have since stopped participating because things here are just done on paper and not in real life.

This thing went on to include a schedule for the monthly breakfast and snack rotation? Where does she get this shit from? She probably pulls it out her fat nasty ass. She concludes the letter, "If you have a concern or any questions, please see me personally or join the team to support school-wide efforts. However, please do not send a response email regarding this correspondence." She knew it was coming—she knew that people would have a problem with this email. She is so unhappy.

Let me sidebar for a moment. No one cited the SOP when a monetary collection was taken up for her birthday and she received a Pandora bracelet from those who contributed. I was not asked to contribute. Had I been, I probably would have had some choice words. When they put that dead tree on her door and passed out apples to write a message to her, I didn't know about that. So, I would say yeah—I was excluded.

I love how she picks apart things that do not benefit or highlight her. She cannot see someone shine, even for a little bit. She is so miserable that evil just encamps around her. No wonder this school is a sinking ship and a ticking time bomb.

Oh, we had our faculty meeting yesterday. I left before it got good. I heard one of the classy colleagues acknowledged the assistant principal through a serenade, letting him know that he is a star. During the rendition, I'm told that The Cow never once looked up. She carried on as if she was actually doing some work. Then, the assistant principal asked for everyone to come take a picture with him. I'm told that The Cow left the room. I'm told she couldn't even fake it any more. The love in the room was so strong and consuming that the hatred and evil had to flee. "Satan, get thee hence." Too funny!!

Day 80:

The dark cloud that hovers over the building subsided, but only for a time. It's Friday and this week of appreciation for our assistant principal, the real MVP has come to a close. Although we planned to do the walking taco bar for him, this was foiled due to her shady letter. We didn't really worry with it since we would take our MVP out right after school. AND we wore our bow ties again today. Yay us, right?

How about this dark cloud came back with lightening vengeance? She pulled the MVP in a meeting right after school. He had to work with the special education teachers, having what I see as an impromptu meeting right after school. Really? On a Friday? This thing is out of control. Her life is so miserable. So, so, so miserable.

I'm sitting here wondering when Karma will pay her ass a special visit. Then, I quietly remember that she is being reminded of her Karma every day. I often ponder from whence comes The Cow's disposition of misery. Perhaps the rumor of her family being dysfunctional is a truth that propels her to lash out at the familial atmosphere I nurture with my class. Or maybe The Cow is so upset with her decreasing beauty and increasing weight that she seeks to eliminate beauty emanating from youthful smiles and glowing faces on our students. This would explain why she often buries her face in fast food instead of burying her anger for anyone in this school who sees hope where she is blind. Her unhappiness attempts to dim the optimism of the educational staff that are here to inspire. I just can't see how she can be blessed, with the type of hatred she has in her heart. She shows up as a miserable beast.

Day 81:

Some days I feel like these last few days could be a breeze and then there are the days like today that make you want to say, "fuck it" and just take it how it comes. In trying to help a situation, I was sucked into the Spawn of Satan's web. This child needs help and it's difficult to separate that or even think that when a child strikes you. Oh yeah, it was one of those days. Not only was I kicked, when I left to go back and attend to my class, this child ran past me and hit me as she flew by. Of course it was intentional.

This is the same child who will try to go "toe-to-toe" with an adult. I have been in the middle of this child going after someone or trying to leave without permission and in telling her not to touch me, she will defiantly touch you softly and say, "I touched you—now what?" Oh, you just don't know how much restraint kicks in to remember that she is still a child, one that is growing and learning every single day. And that's putting it nicely. But this was the worst of the days' fiasco.

The Cow called me for a meeting. This time the assistant principal sat in. I was guided to look at my summative evaluation and sign it. Well you already know that this is not going down. I don't trust this sneaky thing and to think I will sign something in the midst of this storm without thoroughly dissecting it—she is out her rabid ass mind.

I'm trying to understand the logic in her now giving me all threes on this summative—when the formative, just a few weeks ago, had a two for professionalism and another two for communication. I know she is retaliating against me—but the way she is trying to justify it is fucked up. I guess she though that me seeing three's now will have me sign without reading. Um, no. Pump your breaks you fat tub of lard.

I read it. I did. And she is still being sneaky and condescending by suggesting that my absences weren't documented. I will not sign off on anything; especially when I know that you are trying to set me up. Oh, and her biggest piece of the game-was her noting that the PDP was attached (which it wasn't) and citing the PDP for professionalism, communication and attendance. Well, wait now. Wait a damn minute. I have the paperwork you initially submitted-that's not what you said.

She asked if I signed it and I expressed that I would not because I am unclear about the language used in the summative. I pointed out the unattached document but the mention of it being in the evaluation. She suggested that it would be uploaded. Well do your thing fat ass. I'll wait.

Day 82:

I hate that this Cow takes up so much space in my head and so much time from my day. I am in a position where I must anticipate the next move and really advocate for myself. This lady is pure crazy and evil.

The Spawn of Satan told her other teacher that I slapped her. I immediately emailed the child's social worker and guardian. In doing so, I wanted to ensure that I am documenting the things that took place. Because of this, I knew that Division of Family and Children Services (DFACS) would have to intervene and investigate. No problem.

Toward the end of the day, The Cow waddled to my room, wanting to see me in the front. I already knew what it was about. She thought she had something on me. Wouldn't she love to? Since I didn't have any coverage for my students, she sent for her slug. I grabbed my things because they can't be trusted. So, The Cow stated that she would tell me what it was about as we walked down the hall. I don't trust her.

I proceeded to walk ahead of her. Due to her enormous size and shabby knees, this wasn't a difficult task. I entered the "parent liaison" room, where The Cow has established this as her barn. There was a DFACS special investigator there to speak to me about the students' allegations.

We conversed thoroughly. I noted the students' consistently disruptive behaviors, her academic strengths and addressed the allegations. These allegations are the same allegations that frequently come up against a teacher who is at odds with this cow of an administrator. No big deal. As I look at this time of year, this is the same thing that happened to me last year, with another student. Of course The Cow was notified by the Board that the allegations were unsupported, yet she attempted to hold them over my head—well into this school year. My addressing them to her in front of her supervisor is what stopped her from bringing it up. So yeah, this lady is troublesome, to say the least.

After the meeting ended, I returned to my classroom. I refused to be in the same room with the student and made it a point to bring the school counselor into the situation. She was unaware of what was happening in the building, which is something The Cow does to a lot of the people in administrative positions. They know very little, until shit hits the fan or they are informed by someone else.

One of the school counselors came to get the student, however The Cow suggested that the student had to return to class. I remained in the hallway until the student left. The field of education is a fucked-up place to be in, when you teach in underserved schools. The highly respectable level of care, compassion and concern isn't there. Often times we see on social media children disrespecting staff members and even fighting them. A teacher is left to defend themselves against allegations or even abuse (whether verbal or physical). What happens to the child/student? A lot of times nothing.

After this meeting, I was called in for another meeting with The Cow. This time, she had more of the same paperwork. She keeps highlighting the same unfounded issues. I keep questioning the validity of the information contained with the documents, yet she provides nothing. She expects me to sign off on documents that are incomplete and untrue. When I acknowledge the errors and am still asked to sign, my refusal is seen as insubordination. How?

How is it that we are expected to work in such hostile environments and remain effective? How long can we be expected to succumb to abuse from students and lack of support from vindictive administrators and the people who cover for them? When does it become something that is worthy of investigating? When does it become newsworthy?

I ask these questions because it seems that no one really wants to do their job and consider the issues that are taking place in this school and I'm sure in other schools that fail to provide a union (or a level of protection/support) for its workers. We are not protected. We are basically left to defend ourselves from allegations at every angle, including those of irate parents who sometimes refuse to take accountability for their errs, from abusive students who know (subconsciously or not) that they are protected and often times from the administrators who have chosen to forget about the arduous tasks of educating as they collect their six figure salaries. When our voice is strong enough to effect change, that voice becomes the example, whereby others become scared because they aren't prepared for such a battle.

How can I be an effective teacher, when my days are clouded with wanting to protect my certifications and defend my character? Had I been any lesser person, I might have fucked her up already. I'm really trying to be on some Namaste shit and do it right. But I'm really being pushed to a point that even I don't like. Will that be newsworthy then?

The fact is that we are doomed. The county doesn't care because the parents don't care. Nothing happens when parents are uninvolved. So many people run to the "other" schools, screaming they want the best for their child. That's understood. But the best for your child comes when a parent actively participates and ensures that the school functions the way it is supposed to.

How many times have I stayed after school, for a PTA meeting and the majority (if not the only) people in attendance are the teachers? Not only this, why does "leadership" schedule so many things in one night. How can you have parent teacher conferences from 3:15 until 5:15, expect to have a school program and a PTA meeting all in one night? That's too long of a day, for anyone, plus parents may be at work. It is my sincere reasoning that this is by design. These meetings are scheduled the way that they are, to discourage participation. How else can a person think that this even mirrors right action? It doesn't.

This school is failing, flawed, fucked up (or whatever other way you want to say it), because no one cares. The main people that should care—they are the missing piece to the equation. Nothing can change without parent support and participation. How can you, as a parent, expect someone to care more for your child than you? We have got to do better.

Day 83:

As the saga continues, I am prepared to send another letter to the board and whoever else I can think to send my letters to. I'm awaiting call backs from someone at the Atlanta Journal Constitution (AJC) and WSBTV. The first person at WSBTV stated that it sounds like my "boss" is a jerk but it wasn't newsworthy. I really wanted to get my story to Amy Napier Viteri, however she moved to Miami. She was the news anchor that covered the story of other teachers from this same county, but different school, when their principal harassed and bullied them. That principal was fired if I am not mistaken, but definitely removed from the school.

Day 84:

I've always had a "love-hate relationship" with cafeteria workers and secretaries. Why? Because they are mean for what appears to be no fucking reason. There is no reason for you to scream on a small child for not having money on their lunch account. In case they don't know, the children don't have any money. Unless it's some exceptional circumstance, they can't make money to provide for themselves.

One morning, while I had early morning hall duty, I remember a young student (possibly kindergarten) leave the cafeteria in full tears. I stopped him and asked, "What's the matter with you?" He let out a burst of noise and said, "They won't gimme no breakfast." Thinking it might be his siblings, his friends or even an older student, I continued to ask who are the "they" in which he is speaking of. The student finally explains that it's one of the ladies in the cafeteria.

I took the student back thru the line and asked one of the cashiers why the student couldn't get any breakfast. The student and I were informed by the cashier, "He has to pay. He don't get free lunch and he didn't have no money." The food that the student wanted was sitting right on the cash register. The custodian who heard the initial commotion gave the cashier some coins for the students' breakfast. The custodian reached over and took the breakfast off the register and said, "Here you go little buddy."

The custodian later told me that the woman had snatched the students breakfast tray and told him if he didn't have any money he couldn't have the breakfast food. The custodian further explained that after the students touch the food tray, they can't give it to another student but the food becomes trash, which is why the food remained at the register. This makes me so annoyed. We would rather throw away food than to feed a hungry child. It makes very little sense.

I remember when I first began teaching in the public school system. I started off as a kindergarten teacher at a Title 1 school in an amazing county on the East Coast. I had a student named after a city in Colorado. A bright and happy student who could read just about anything you gave her. She was one student who brought her lunch daily or her parents occasionally paid for her lunch. Her parents ensured that her lunch account had money on it from week to week to cover the days she would eat at school.

As with our normal routine, I would walk my students to the cafeteria and place them in line to which the staff on cafeteria duty would take over the guidance of the students. From there, I would go have lunch or make copies or complete whatever tasks I needed for the day. I remember sitting in my classroom and seeing my student enter the classroom crying. I had never seen her cry and much less couldn't remember her ever being sad, so I was very concerned. She showed me a paper that the cafeteria worker had given her, which stated that she had to eat a cold cheese sandwich because she didn't have enough money to have a warm cafeteria meal.

This was my first real encounter, as a teacher, with an insolent "cafeteria lady." I was furious. I didn't really know what to do, but I knew that denying a small child a meal was plain wrong. The student and I went to the cafeteria worker and I inquired about the meal and whether the child could have a "real" meal. The cafeteria lady denied me as well. She mentioned that the older children come through the line all the time with promises to pay and never pay. I explained that its different for a smaller child, not to mention she typically has money on her account. I further tried to reason that the mother of this child would definitely pay the money back. This lady wouldn't budge.

I went to my friend and mentor, who was the school counselor. She mentioned that the principal had acknowledge that every student should eat a warm meal and that money was in the school budget to cover those who needed lunch money. With my student tagging along, I went to my principal and he confirmed that he had money for these incidents. He immediately wrote a note asking the cafeteria lady to keep a record of how much money is owed and he would cut a check at the end of the week to cover any deficit. Amazing!

I happily took my hand-written note from the principal to give to the cafeteria lady. She reluctantly accepted the note. Little did I know that this would be the start of my "love-hate relationship" with cafeteria workers. Why the fuck are you mad that the children can get a warm meal? Why are most of y'all so damn mean and ornery? I can't understand it. I burned up my entire lunch break but I was able to help my student get a warm lunch! From this day on, I began to eat lunch with my students so that I knew that they would be treated respectfully.

Yes, true, I know it's not every cafeteria worker, because I have met some awesome and caring food service workers. It's really the few within the group that makes it difficult on the rest. It's to those few that I shake my head and worry about the condition of your hearts. Just mean, rude and selfish. It doesn't have to be that way.

We are in a title one school, a failing “focus” school. Many of the children in this building receive some sort of free or reduced lunch. These children are usually in somewhat “impoverished” households, probably receiving some sort of government assistance. Why would you deprive a child, in this situation, of a hot meal? Sure, they give them a “courtesy” meal which consists of a cold cheese sandwich on white bread and some milk. Really? How is this appropriate? And then you charge them for the “courtesy” meal? What sense does this make?

This year, one of my students goes through the line only to come out at the cash register and be demeaned. The student reaches the nasty cafeteria staff and is reprimanded for not having money in her account. There has to be a better way. The child has already breathed on the food and now you snatch it out her little hands? How is this justice or fairness or right action?

I’m sure there is more than enough food left over at the end of the lunch period. Where does this food go? There are children who are absent each day, what about the count for their lunch? What about the food that is inevitably thrown away? And there isn’t enough for this child to get a freaking lunch? You have got to be kidding me?

My students spirit was broken. Initially, I ignored it because I have so much shit on my plate as is that I cannot fight her battle too. Then I got mad at myself. When did I lose my damn compassion for advocating for children? How in the hell can I think that I can overlook a crying child that only wants to eat a meal? I can't. I asked the child what she had on her tray and I would buy it for her. She refused. I asked her to let me buy her something to eat, she again refused. This made me furious because they truly succeeded at breaking her spirit. I stood up and went to see about getting her some food.

Well actually, I went to curse some muthafuckas out. Seriously! I was very upset and very much prepared to just quit. If I can't be compassionate, if my passion has dwindled to nothingness and turning away from what's right, if I can't advocate for the right thing to do…then I need to get the hell on. In that moment, I was ready to do just that. My assistant principal intervened and handled it.

Public school is a joke. Well this is clearly a blanket statement. I can't judge every single school by this one—but it's so hard not to. This whole system of education is corrupt, especially in this county. Lost accreditation, several superintendents rotating in and out, regional/area superintendents covering for principals, principals unfulfilled and miserable. Shit just keeps rolling downhill.

I have officially given up on public school education and their shenanigans. Should I make it through the end of this school year, I salute the building and tell the principal to kiss my whole ass. Should I not make it, please set aside some bail money for me.

Day 85:

My version of the tune: "Ain't No sunshine" by Bill Withers

"There's so much sunshine when she's gone/she's the dark cloud and she's away/there's so much sunshine when she's gone/cause this Cow just a big ole storm/whenever she rolls this way."

A little humor on my morning. Each day seems exceptionally difficult, coming into a place that doesn't feed the spirit of a person who wants to do what's right. It's so painful and it feels like a slow death. No one should ever have to feel this way.

While I understand that I am powerful beyond measure and I know that my cup is half full, there are moments. This school year has been filled with plenty of them. My only motivation is the completion of this book and collecting my summer check from this hell hole. Outside of these connections to the school I have nothing else to give. This school, this situation, has drained me and has attempted to break my spirit but I will be victorious.

Day 86:

Days off mean so much, especially when returning to this jungle. Then there is standardized testing on a Monday. It's crazy up in this place. It's as if the children are anxious, just as we are, for this upcoming summer break. With only a few weeks left of school I kinda wish we could do them all back-to-back and get the hell on.

These weekends only tease me and make me even more frustrated when I return.

The Cow hobbled down the halls, peaking in classrooms. This is the most she walks in the building—testing and observation time. Maybe we should have more standardized testing and observations because, considering everything else, she needs all the movement she can get. I mean, if not-they will surely send her to slaughter. The biggest cows are the ones to go first. Doesn't she know that? Mooooooooooo!

Day 87:

This place is literally killing me. My blood pressure has sky rocketed. I'm looking at the numbers like damn, should I even go to work today. Then I'm thinking of this stupid PDP and how I am trying to hang in there until the last day of school. Be stellar. Damn, but will I make it?

I swear, if it weren't for my family and finances I would have been told this fat bitch to kiss my ass and kept it pushing. I'm a little frustrated with myself that my "peace of mind" savings is at war with itself. I know better next time. Actually, there won't be a next time. This will never happen again. I will never allow it.

I do know that I am going to have to step my exercise routine up a notch. I am going to do this smoothie cleanse and log all of my food. I have to hit it hard from every angle because this stress is something that is unavoidable. Even when I am quiet, she still fucks with me. So why not go hard on her fat ass. So every time she sees me it's on.

As I look around my classroom, I realize how disgusted I am. I'm disgusted that this school system continues to go through so many changes that the children have been forgotten. I'm disgusted that the people who have these advanced degrees are so far removed from classroom instruction that they have not one clue with what we deal with on the battlefields of educating these children. I'm disgusted that ignored cries and pleas have been silenced and no one hears the most necessary voices. I'm disgusted that these standardized tests continue to divide us and it's done so purposely. I'm disgusted with the system.

I'm disgusted that this cow of a principal can sit high and attempt to look "low." I'm disgusted that karma hasn't bit her ass. I'm disgusted that she can get away with unprofessional behaviors. I'm disgusted that she can run away great educators and not be held accountable. I'm disgusted that I have to see her damn face. I'm disgusted with this unpleasant, micromanaging, self-serving, cowardly, self-righteous, manipulative, ill-equipped, antagonistic, injudicious, blame and fault finding, evil, guileful, passive-aggressive, methodical, corrupt, ruthless, classless, deceptive, malicious, condescending, sneaky, ornery, hateful, vindictive, so-called principal.

I'm disgusted at the children who will be passed on to 2nd Grade, and there is nothing I can do about it. I'm disgusted that some of these 1st Graders were promoted when they were ill prepared for this level of work. I'm disgusted that the behaviors in the classroom are atrocious and there isn't support from the so-called administration. I'm disgusted and disappointed that children, at this age, have no real understanding or value of education. I'm disgusted that children lack respect for adults.

I'm disgusted that parents aren't concerned, enough, about the education of their children. I'm disgusted that they lack enough love to give their child the very best, aside from material bullshit. Children coming in here day in and day out with the latest Jordan sneakers and colorful Kevin Durant's, yet your child is reading below kindergarten level. Even at the end of the year your child hasn't learned shit? What is the point of calling yourself a parent?

I'm disgusted that the classroom rules aren't reinforced in home life. A parent can sit their child in front of an app but not one that's educational. Oh, the children talk about all their gadgets but rarely do they share with me a new book they have received. I'm disgusted that I am still in this school, still sitting at my desk counting days down. I'm disgusted that I am not courageous enough to pack my shit and walk the fuck out. I'm just disgusted.

Day 88:

Summative evaluations are being signed off on, and some teachers are a bit pissed. The snakeish behavior of The Cow strikes again. I'm contemplating whether I should sign off on it or add a nice/nasty note with it. On the one hand, if I sign it adding the comments that I want I will be looked at as unprofessional, perpetuating the lies that this cow has told. If I don't sign it, I still run the risk of looking unprofessional and her comments go in as if my only reason for not signing it is because it's probably true. So really no matter what I do, I am going to be considered (or looked at as) the trouble maker.

I wrote out some comments to add to the summative evaluations, just in case. I'm contemplating adding it, but my sister Ashanti told me it was too emotional. Well, it's the truth.

> "Many of my days missed were prior to accepting my first-grade class. My absences are due to health concerns which have been documented with doctor's [proof]. It was suggested that I request Family and Medical Leave Act (FMLA), which I have done. I am still in the process of having this paperwork approved. Furthermore, the hours/days in which you suggest that I have missed are incorrect. I have submitted this information to you on March 10th for your

review. Yet, you have not acknowledged this information, yet again.

My concern is that your retaliatory actions against me are as a result of my letters to the board. You, Dr. [cow], continue to ignore the documents that I have submitted to you. Attempts to speak to you are regarded as "unprofessional" when in fact you are the one person who is unprofessional. The way in which you speak to adults is very demeaning, condescending and strategic. However, certain people such as myself [have] been called unprofessional because I defend myself against your attacks and slander. In meetings, you quickly write that I am refusing to sign documents, when in fact I have shared with you several times the documents you sent to me are incorrect (such as the summative you wanted me to sign off on April 18th, which stated that a document was attached and I noted that there was nothing attached). You have also refused to allow me to sign off on notes that you have taken in a meeting, when it was suggested by [your supervisor] that we sign off on each other's notes. You have disregarded several requests by [your supervisor]. Is that not unprofessional?

The "meetings" that you call to discuss the bogus PDP that you have attempted to place me on is further acknowledgement that you attempt to destroy any person who questions your motives and seeks clarity for the misrepresentations with your "leadership." In said meetings, you continue to invite your [minion maggot], who is known throughout the building to be just as deceptive as you are. Your track record, in this school, with teachers who have been at the helm strategically manipulated and calculated harassment is lengthy. It remains a mystery as to why it hasn't been investigated further. Or is it?"

Too much? I don't know. But the truth is the truth. Just like my facial expressions can reveal my entire mood, I think writing reveals a whole lot. But it's a whole lot of truth. What can I say?

Day 89:

Early this morning, my paraprofessional gets hauled out by the ambulance. It was such a show-for The Cow. She wanted me to leave my classroom and receive the students elsewhere. I don't really care, but know that I won't leave my personal belongings in the same room with her. So I grabbed my water, my green smoothie, my purse and my backpack, locked my computer only for her to tell me never mind. Whatever!

Then, when the paramedics arrived, she asked me to leave out. I said nothing, grabbed all my essential things, yet again and gathered my students who were randomly placed in other classrooms. I told the school counselor to have my children come into the classroom across from mine. It just happened to be my "Black Power Twin" as we have been so affectionately named.

I knew this would make The Cow mad because she is always making references to her about me and making references to me about her. I don't care what this cow has to say, she is really a "non-motherfucking factor." Wasn't that the popular catchphrase? Yea, that.

So when it was time to re-enter my classroom, The Cow hid by the side of the classroom door and sent someone to do her work. My "twin" and I embraced one another and offered words of encouragement for the day. I've heard this makes the devil mad. She was livid. She snatched a sign off my "twin's" door. The sign was asking that people are quiet as her children were taking the Georgia Kindergarten Inventory of Developing Skills (GKIDS) test. Of course they weren't testing at that time but she had the sign up in preparation. She didn't know that my paraprofessional would have to be wheeled out on a stretcher and that I would be held up in her classroom.

I didn't realize that tampering with someone's belongings was appropriate. How professional! I mean, really, what purpose did it serve? This thing is just hateful solely to be hateful. Can her life be that miserable that she brings her wrath to this place? Probably.

Guess who is now on a PDP? Yup, my "twin" is on a PDP and in the several emails that have gone back and forth, The Cow denied taking the sign? Really? I sat there and watched her snatch it off the door. She is on camera. But my thought is, "Why snatch it off the door in the first place"? The problem is that the emails going back and forth are documentation. She stays away from documentation, she is clever. A detestable person, but clever nonetheless.

Here we are with one teacher being investigated for allegedly scratching a student. Meanwhile this is the same student that comes to school, fights and disrupts the class. I don't know if the teacher did it or not, but I do know the students word is questionable. So they move the student out of this teachers' classroom and places the child in another class-where this teacher has about 27 students, already! This is a mess.

Let's add to this mess, with one of my students punching my "twin" in the stomach three times, today. The Cow doesn't want the parent to be spoken to and has done everything she can to avoid allowing the parent and my "twin" to connect. This is a madhouse. So teachers can be the punching bags and nothing happens-in fact the children can remain in school? The minute there is an allegation—then the world stops and the child is catered to. What the what?

This same student (a student in my class), assaulted a teacher and is the same student who called me a bitch during his first day of class. Upon entering my classroom, I went to introduce myself to him. He didn't say much or even acknowledge my presence. He didn't want to leave his mother and began to cry. I attempted to calm him down and let him know that everything would be alright. I held out my hand as a gesture to let him know that I was friendly and I said, "It's okay. Come in the classroom and let mommy go back to work." Without missing a beat, he looked at me and said, "Shut up, bitch."

I dropped my bitch made hand and simply closed my classroom door. I figured the secretary and the mother could handle it because I didn't know what to do. I just tapped out. All I could think about was here comes another one. Later that day, the student became aggressive with the gym teacher and couldn't be consoled. I tried to help. I approached the student with caution and spoke to him kindly. He told me to fuck myself. I politely moved away from him and suggested they get an administrator. I later found out that he called the assistant principal a "punk."

This same student, a first grader, physically assaults a teacher months later. Did I dodge a bullet? The speech pathologist teacher attempted to help him read a book that he previously enjoyed. At some point, the teacher noticed that he was getting agitated. In her attempt to calm him, she got too close. The teacher stated, "He jumped on the table and grabbed me by my hair. The next thing I knew, he jumped from the table, with my hair in his hands and pulled me to the ground." The student was soon on top of her, screaming and pulled her hair to the point that he ripped small patches from her head. She continued to scream until the students, who were in the room, ran to get help. A male teacher was able to pull the student off the teacher and place him in a separate room.

The teacher, who was afraid, came to me to describe the incident and ask what I thought she should do. "I reported it to the front office, but I don't think they will do anything. I'm scared to be in the same room with him. What if no one was there to get me help?" At that very moment, she was paged to come to the front office. I suggested that she write a statement and demand that something be done.

This incident isn't isolated and gives credence that the child is dangerous and needs help. He has issues beyond the scope of what this school can handle. They take in anybody. I know other counties do a thorough screening, you can't bring these vile behaviors to their schools. They have ways and methods of keeping people out.

Day 90:

After a few exchanges with The Cow, my "black power twin" wanted to speak to the parent of the child who hit her several times. Of course, The Cow is striving to block this meeting/conference/exchange. Today, I noticed that The Cow walked the parent and child to class as the student entered late. When does this naturally happen? Rarely-if ever. This cow is up to something, as always.

I heard that she was mad that I called 911, yesterday, for the teacher that was having difficulty standing and focusing. I'm sure she thought this was something other than what it was. I'm told she was mad that someone came to the room before she could waddle down the hall. Well, no one is going to wait for her to walk faster or even have compassion.

How about by the end of the day there is a call for several people including myself, to come sign off on the summative evaluation. Here we go again. I'm not going to rush. For what? After consulting with my husband and my cousin (who is an assistant principal in a different state), I was encouraged to send an email to The Cow and her supervisor. In this way, I can document that I did not refuse to sign the summative evaluation, but that it will be signed once the corrections are resolved.

No sooner than I draft up my "professional" email-the maggot liar calls me asking if I signed off on my summative evaluation. Oh, I just love how The Cow sends her manure to do her bidding. I mean, I guess that's what happens when a less than qualified person signs up for a role in which they aren't what? *ding, ding, ding* QUALFIED! Any who, she calls me asking if I signed off on my evaluation. Wait, what? Hello—who are you?

So, I (in my as professional as I can be while being nice/nasty voice) told her that she should look into TKES and see. In like fashion, of her lying ass supervisor, she attempts to change my words. She makes a comment stating, so you didn't sign it. I corrected her swiftly, letting her know that what she said is not what I said. Annoyed, we both are, she asks me again if I signed it. I told her I didn't know and that I would be up there for my conference shortly.

Of course, I take a look at my evaluation—and wouldn't you know, The Cow has changed my three's to two's. It's a miracle. Or is it? Someone must have put their foot in her large back. A person, such as her, doesn't change from being a nasty ass witch to a good Samaritan in just a couple hours. What really happened?

Since I still had comments that were not accurate, I sent my email to her—the assistant principal and the regional superintendent. I packed my things for the evening and went to my meeting. When I got there, I swear I walked into a fog because The Cow was ever so nice and kind. I'm not buying your bullshit, ma'am, sir. What have you done with The Cow? Did you eat her?

In asking if I signed my summative evaluation, I stated that it was not signed because there were some errors. Now she wants to know the errors and wants me to write down the discrepancy. She fumbles on the computer, speaking so kindly. What kind of horror movie is this? Am I being Punk'd? Where is the camera?

She is giggling, informed me that, "Oh, I changed that," and "Oh, let me look at what I wrote," and, "Well write down your cell phone number so I can text you when I update it." Of course she claims to not have been able to access it right now but she will keep working on it. Not buying that shit. But I bet you this won't be signed off. Not right now, not without a rebuttal. Fix my shit.

Day 91:

It's Teacher Appreciation Week!!

Last night I was super excited as I thought about my gift to the teachers who assist me in the classroom. I budgeted and saved in order to give them a gift that I think they will truly appreciate. I gifted all three of them with a massage. They truly deserve it.

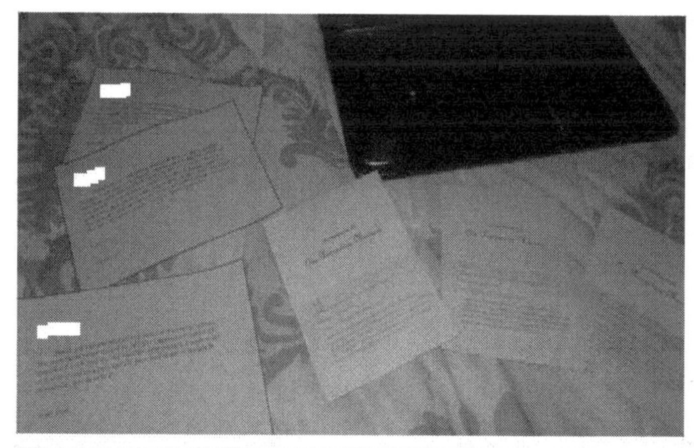

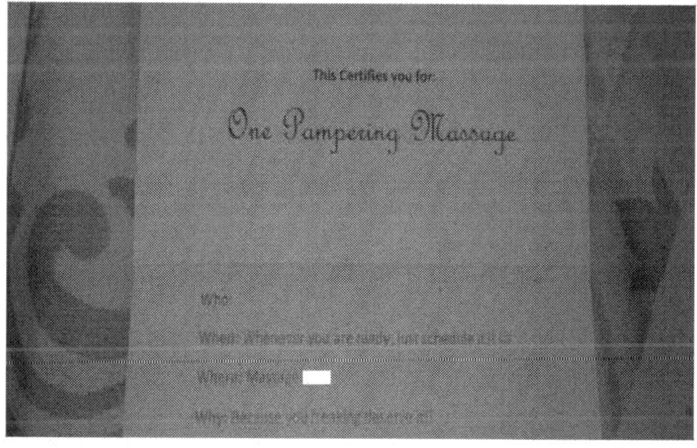

I sat down and wrote them a personalized letter, thanking them for their unique characteristics and skills that they bring to this class. I made them a cute gift card that "certifies" them for one "Pampering Massage." I sat back and just got happy at the thought of going in to work. I miss the days when I was excited to come in and teach my students. I miss being excited about the things I would share, the questions that would be asked and the light bulbs that I helped turn on.

Those days, for now, have been long gone. I am so over this class, this school and this county. For now—I will celebrate the teachers who deserve it and have gratitude for where I am and who I am. I wouldn't have made it this far—had I been a weak and inconsistent sheep.

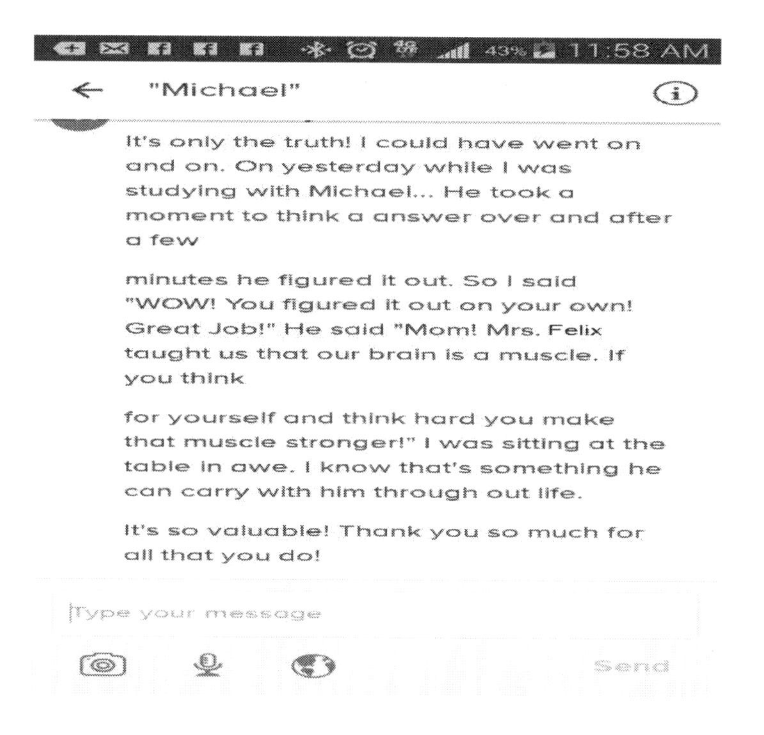

The excitement for the day was short lived. The students seemed even more wound up than usual—or is my patience worn thin? Either way, I was taunted by a CHILD attempting to hit me with a back pack. Just out of control. The Spawn of Satan is back in full effect, as if things had calmed down. I'm just so ready for it to be over.

Day 92:

I was off yesterday and I enjoyed every minute of it. It makes my thoughts of the summer all the more sweeter. I did come back to an earful of information. The substitute teacher questioned how I do this every day. She had to kick the Spawn of Satan out of the classroom and restrain herself from putting her hands on a child. Geez Louise, this is what I deal with every single day.

It's interesting to me that everyone can see this except some people. Then again, I know that it's not wanting to be seen. That cow knows what's going on, the behaviors, in this classroom. This whole school is out of control. Poor leadership kills schools.

Day 93:

Today turned out to be an okay day. I mean, all we did was watch a movie. Because The Cow decided that she will have day long professional developments to go over the "new" format of the lesson plan and the "I Do, We Do, You Do" model of instruction. But wait—didn't this lesson plan change in January some time? It did. And haven't we been teaching this way, off paper and on paper? We have. So what's the point?

See—we have an issue with substitute teachers taking jobs within this building. When they come in, they immediately see how dysfunctional and chaotic it is. They aren't supported because we aren't supported. So when they come in for a day of subbing, many don't return. So, now we have day long professional developments, and no coverage. How smart. Tomorrow 1st Grade has their day and by then, I am sure no substitutes will show up. So who will have this class? It's going to be interesting to find out.

In any event, Kindergarten, 1st Grade, 2nd Grade and 5th Grade showed up to lunch at the same time. This is because the schedule was made from someone who lacks insight into instruction and planning. Can you imagine the confusion? The long lines, the noise, the lack of space. It was crazy. We were sent back to our classrooms, only to be called right back. The lines were completely backed up. I thoroughly enjoyed seeing The Cow dazed and confused. She didn't know how to handle the students that we are tasked to service each day. She hasn't a clue.

Oh, and there was a news article written that informed us that our school remains on the list for "takeover" based on the governor's proposal. Am I surprised? Nah!

Day 94:

What a day, what a day, what a day.

First, a teacher gets snatched up by the bully cow (principal), then I'm assaulted by a habitually violent first grader and now (as I write this) I'm sitting in the doctor's office, attempting to collect my thoughts on the events of the day.

Okay, so I'm walking thru the halls and I see one of my colleagues frantic. I walk over to see what the commotion was about and she shows me her bruised right arm. She proceeds to tell me that The Cow attempted to force a conversation with her.

Now let me pause for the cause and remind you that this is what the heifer does. She bullies and bulldozes her way into a conversation with a person, even when she is asked not to and has been asked not to (this is documented in an email that was sent to us both by her supervisor). She has done me like this several times. Okay, so The Cow is upset at my colleague (let's call her "*Smiles*"), for whatever reasons the evil voices in her head tell her. The latest was that a student allegedly told The Cow that *Smiles* and another colleague were talking about the size of The Cow.

Okay, run that back. The Cow…brought third party information (gossip, mess, pettiness)…that was allegedly from a child (an innocent student, an unsuspecting minor, our youth)…to a teacher (a colleague, a respectful adult, a classy lady). The Cow is said to have stated that she (The Cow) responded to the child stating something to the effect that *Smiles* (the one she assaulted) didn't have room to talk. Say what?? So *Smiles* mentioned to The Cow that she never said anything about her, especially to or in front of a child.

Fast forward a few days. I guess The Cow felt the need to speak to *Smiles* in private. In attempting to force *Smiles* into a conversation, *Smiles* politely declined speaking to this bully in private and cited that she didn't feel comfortable. As old habits die hard, the bully cow heifer grabbed *Smiles* by her arm and snatched her toward her. Say what?? I saw the bruise with my own two eyes and pictures have been taken of the red, swollen and torn skin.

As I hear the story, I'm wondering why shit like this doesn't happen to me. Because for real…I would have rolled that big bitch. Oh, pardon me…I would have politely asked her not to physically touch me in that manner, as it is not polite and offends me ever so greatly. Nah, that just doesn't have the same feel as rolling her fat ass. Yea, I woulda rolled her fat ass!!! How about that for "newsworthy".

So, the teacher, my colleague, decided that she needed to go see urgent care. Girl, better you than me because I would have had to call home for bail money. I'm so glad she proactively emailed the superintendent and the regional supervisor. Let's see how they cover this shit up. Because we do know this will be covered up, right? (side eye)

Alright, so on to me being physically assaulted. I had an irate student that attempted to disrespect every student in my classroom.

She, the Spawn of Satan, ultimately became so upset because the students she attempted to bully turned the tables on her. Yea!

So as I attempted to diffuse the situation—I asked the little habitually violent and disruptive student to leave the classroom. Of course she refused. I went to her desk to assist her out of the classroom. She declined. I picked her up and carried her to the classroom door. At this point, with three adults witnessing and the entire class, she kicked me twice in my shin. Oh, the agony!!!

The Spawn of Satan kicked me in the same area for which I am currently being seen at the VA. I had a previous injury from my days of military physical training, otherwise known as PT. I've been avoiding any type of cutting and surgery because I intend to keep full use of my limbs and the VA has a way of practicing on veterans—many leaving in far worse condition than they came. No surgery for me. In the meantime, they just offer pain management. I manage just fine with ice and occasional heat therapy.

I solicited the help of another teacher who escorted her to another room. I was called a bastard and other choice words that I dare not repeat (oh, the offense thrown). I had to clutch my pearls!! I was in pain and now with a slight limp.

I so wanted to call the police. Instead I made a fuss to the pseudo administrator, the bald maggot. She was no help, as I knew she would be. She can't be trusted. Her main role is to lick ass to maintain a position that she hasn't earned. I digress. But the message was loud and clear…I'm calling the po-po (aka police).

I emailed The Cow and her supervisor. I was responded to immediately, despite me previously calling and walking to her temporary bomb shelter, where she was not hiding. I swear, there must be a trap door in that damn room. I literally called then walked to the same room I called and neither the bald maggot nor The Cow were out to pasture. Well, I'll be a monkeys' uncle. Next thing I know, I get an email and I see the "how now brown cow" done waddled down the hall to my room. Interesting seeing you here, welcome!!!

She told me to fill out an incident report form. She was ever so kind in assisting me with the wrong paperwork. This is what she does, she likes to intentionally withhold information or provide the wrong information. I read it, it said <u>not</u> for teacher incidents, but I filled it out anyway (because clearly, she thinks I'm stupid) …got a signature and my copies. Yea, you have to ensure that these people do their job, hold 'em accountable. You going to the doctor? Damn straight I am. This is not a game. I'm already under doctor's care for a military injury and this thang might have aggravated it. Oh, the agony!!!

This place…this whole place is hell. Hellish behaviors, hellish "principal," hellish process. HELLementary.

Day 95:

As I enter the building, I'm greeted with a message about not being afforded the opportunity to attend a training that correlates with the new lesson plan. I'm told that the teachers who are planning to return for the upcoming school year will get first priority. Good luck with that.

I'm trying to figure out how it was determined to be a good idea to bring in a training at the END of the school year. We literally have a couple weeks left in this school year. Not only that, the template to the lesson plan changed months ago—so we have been teaching based on that format. I mean I am all for additional resources, but I cannot understand how it is beneficial to have this training now. There are exactly 14 school days before summer. This school is unorganized and I see why we are failing in so many areas.

The day was chaotic, like all the others. Since substitute teachers didn't pick up, students were merged into already full classes. Teachers that teach enrichment classes (such as art, music and math/science lab) were now the substitute teachers. So that meant we didn't get a planning period. We also had to eat with our students. Oh, and The Cow created a schedule that was all the way fucked up. She thought it would be a good idea to have 5th Grade, kindergarten, first and second grade come to lunch at the same time as well as invite the teachers to get some taco buffet that was prepared for them (because I refuse to eat from the hands of people who are evil). Wait a minute now!

On any given day, our cafeteria staff cannot handle the load of one class at a time, without an overflow. It's amazing that people who set out to make schedules (and decisions) for us aren't even aware of what goes on, on a day-to-day basis.

Happy Teachers Appreciation Day to us all.

Day 96:

Another day with minimal coverage, children dispersed, teachers in all day trainings-still behind the 8 Ball. This building is beyond crazy. I found some data that supports it.

One thing I can see is that the College and Career Ready Performance Index (CCRPI) has declined each year since 2012. While the CCRPI replaced the previous year's Adequate Yearly Progress (AYP) measurement within the No Child Left Behind (NCLB), I can bet that AYP has declined since The Cow has been here. It's been verbally stated—but I need solid evidence. I mean, we all know she is garbage, but will the data prove it? I'm sure it will.

On the governor's website, the Opportunity School District (OSD) proposal states, "In order to turn around struggling schools, Gov. Nathan Deal proposed creation of an Opportunity School District. Based on similar, successful initiatives in Louisiana and Tennessee, it would authorize the state to temporarily step in to assist chronically failing public schools and rescue children languishing in them.

- In the governor's proposal, persistently failing schools are defined as those scoring below 60 on the Georgia Department of Education's accountability measure, the College and Career Performance Index, for three consecutive years.
- The OSD would take in no more than 20 schools per year, meaning it would govern no more than 100 at any given time.
- Schools would stay in the district for no less than five years but no more than 10 years, and would then return to local control."

According to the document ("Schools Eligible for Opportunity School District-OSD"), which is posted on the same website, any score below 60 is considered to be an "F" or failing. This school has failed three years in a row. There is also data that supports that this school was at 61.6% (near failing) in the year 2012.

In correlation with an email that was sent by the superintendent, "nearly all OSD schools are on track to leave the list." The email stated that there were six schools that are expected to be off the list within one-two years, another 13 schools that are expected to be off the list within two-three years, and three schools that are in need of "intensive, enhanced assistance and services." Wait!! This school isn't even on the list? This place is so bad it's pretty much on life support and can probably expect to have the cord pulled as soon as the family is notified.

So again, why is it that no one heard the declarations of the teachers crying for help? Do they care? If they can't care enough to ensure that the teacher's needs are being met how certain can we be that they are caring for the needs of the students in which they claim to service?

Day 97:

The Cow walked a parent down to my class. I saw them peeking in my room as I taught my English/Language Arts lesson. Yes, my students were definitely engaged and learning. She would love to catch me not doing something. She can hold her breath.

In my mind, I knew this was the start of some bullshit. Yesterday the lady who transports the Spawn of Satan told me that the guardian wants to report me. When I inquired for the reason, she said HIPPA violation. Well, I told this particular lady that she can go ahead and report me because I broke no such law.

In any event, The Cow escorted a parent, so we will see how it unfolds. This parent came in and began speaking about the child and I immediately asked her relationship to the child. We spoke about the child's behavior and upcoming events that the child would not be participating in. After shooting the breeze, she attempted to size me up. She asked if I were a first-year teacher. Well, thank you for the complement on my youthful appearance, but no I am 10 years strong in this. Surprise!

I like how people want to intimidate others with their knowledge or skill base. Maybe it wasn't intimidation, it could just be one flexing or strutting their stuff. Regardless, none of that matters much to me. You can be retired, as she was, and still have little clue as to what I have seen within the field. Hell, with this class. She basically tried to share with me that my 10 years is nothing and that this situation is preparing me for the next lesson in life. I like that, but please check your ego at the door. You really don't know me or my background, for that matter. We ended the conversation well, she flexed and I flexed right back. She strutted and I strutted. I can match your ego with my wits. No problem.

This day was pretty much like all others. Impatience and frustration is thick. I'm still counting the days down. I'm also looking forward to the conference call that I have been invited on. The Teacher Defense System is "Bringing JUSTICE Back to the Teachers." I am all for that. I am looking to get more information. I do know that movement of helping teachers understand their rights is so very necessary.

Day 98:

What continues to amaze me is how parents will damn near come to blows over their child not attending field day activities, but when it's time to use that same energy for your child's academics you are nowhere to be found. Really?

I sent out a message to the parents of students who would not be allowed to attend field day activities due to their consistently disruptive behaviors. Of course, these aren't behaviors that just happen sporadically, these are behaviors that happen damn near daily. I have documented behaviors through ClassDojo[5], their daily agenda as well as through text messages. Then that one text message, "Your child will not be participating in field day activities due to continuous disruptive behaviors" set shit in motion.

I had a parent tell me that they don't check dojo and that I should have called. No, ma'am, what you should do is be a bit more proactive in your parental responsibilities so that you know what is

---

[5] ClassDojo is a communication app for the classroom. It connects teachers, parents and students who use it to share photos, videos and messages through the day. They use ClassDojo to work together as a team, share in the classroom experience, and bring big ideas to life in their classrooms and homes. (https://www.classdojo.com/about/)

going on with your child. Your child has an "N" for conduct, yet you still don't know? I sent home a conference sheet, which I fill out for each of my students, even when parents don't show up for the scheduled school-wide conference. In this document, a month ago, I mentioned the same thing. So, again, you don't know what's going on in this classroom, and with your child because you are choosing not to know. To take it even further, your child is in the first grade…cannot read, and doesn't know a lot of sounds and blends to even read sight words.

How long have we been doing this? And you still don't know your child's strengths and weaknesses? What? Am I supposed to go home with your child too? I can't do everything for you. I won't. I'm doing my portion and you, parent ma'am, need to do yours as well. But then again, rationalizing with illogical thinking "parents" is like fighting an unrealistic war. I just can't.

My biggest and only concern through all this is the lack of support from The Cow. She avoids parent complaints and pretty much everything else in this school. I knew getting support from her would be lost. So I prepared myself by printing out all of my documentation from ClassDojo (five months of it) as well as hard copies of the recent report card and conference sheet available. Especially after the father, obviously speaking in front of the older child, said that if his son didn't get field day that no one else would get it either. I'm so not intimidated by those sorts of threats. Not even a little bit. Needless to say, the child didn't come to school-so all of that was for naught.

Field day turned out to be alright. There were a few fights because children couldn't handle the pressure of competition and cried when they lost. The anger with these little children confuses me. They have some severe emotional disturbances and I wonder (in my fleeting thoughts) what is going on in their homes. I shake my head at the thought (SMH)!

Day 99:

We still do not have a date for the school talent show. The teachers who have been organizing it have been asking. Since I plan to be in the talent show, as a special featured act, I need to know what day this will all unfold. But, again, this cow loves to make it as if the teachers are the ones who failed to prepare properly. No, ma'am. I'm looking at your scores and I see the truth.

With today being the last day for field day, my class was packed with my students and other students who could not attend due to behaviors. The day seemed to go by so slow. I am never really amazed at the disruptive behaviors, I am more so amazed, shocked really-with how things are handled. The assistant principal wasn't here, so all those behavior issues were left up to The Cow. She had the nerve to be hidden in the parent liaison room with the window covered. I mean who are we really fooling? We know her real office is a pigsty!

Day 100:

As the days dwindle, so too does my patience. I thought I was ready for this day but then something as simple as these janky computers set me in a mood that was best stated as annoyed. We are supposed to test students using STAR Reading assessment, however the computers take forever to load up. Many of the children still cannot log themselves on. The children begin to test and the internet freezes. Other students couldn't see all the answer options. I mean, come on!!

By the time every student gets on the computer and gets in a groove we have to shut everything down to go to lunch. It has been a day. Then the new Early Intervention Program (EIP) teacher brings around some papers that need to be completed by the day's end. No training? Oh, so you get what you get. I did my best. (side eye)

I'm so ready for these last few days. I can't even think straight. I'm looking at the calendar, then looking at the remaining days and I remember when we were in the hundreds. So glad these double digits have rolled up on me. I can't even say it has gone fast, because it hasn't. I have felt every day, hour, minute, second of this hell hole. I look forward to it being over!

Day 101:

If I could be the voice of some of the highly qualified, passionate, diligent teachers that are here with me, going through hell, they would undoubtedly say that it's not worth the fight. You fight with children, to teach them what their parents don't. You fight with children to teach them the basics, which aren't being reinforced at home. You fight with children to teach them manners and discipline. You fight parents, who refuse to allow their children to be disciplined. You fight parents who would rather you give their child a grade than them allow you to show them the ways that THEY can help their child. You fight against parents to be accountable for the children they brought into this world. You fight against a weak administrator who goes along to get along because in her reclusive state of mind she avoids disagreements with parents, temporarily appeasing them so that she can retreat to her calculated manipulative and divisive ways. You fight against a system that continues to create biased (and soon obsolete) assessments to "assess" the students to no true avail. Or at least we have yet to uncover their true agenda. These tests measure what? Initially, we think the assessment will allow the parent to see the deficiencies in their child-possibly aiding them in obtaining additional assistance or retention to help the child receive what they missed. No—that doesn't work…the parent fights that and the child is promoted. We continue to fight a system that isn't designed with the child in mind. A system that supports an inadequate parent, a failing child and social promotion. Does anyone see why we, as a people, as a race, as a community, as a Nation continue to fall behind?

Well, since I cannot be the voice for the teachers in the trenches, in hell, I will be the loudest voice for myself. This is bullshit—and someone, some THING needs to be held accountable. That only happens when we, as a people, as a race, as a community, as a Nation rise and say enough is enough.

You really have the power. It's your power. It's your right.

Day 102:

You know, I really had planned to perform in the talent show this year. Last year, I was Tina Turner and we brought the "Ike and Tina Revue" out of retirement. I asked four of my Fifth Graders to perform *Proud Mary* with me. One of the students that agreed to perform with me was the same student with whom I had a run in with her mother. The performance was classic. We practiced for about a week. We organized our outfits and even borrowed wigs.

Only a select few of "need to know" people knew specifically what we were doing. Other than that, we kept everything a big secret. On the shows program, we were listed as "special guests." It was awesome! On the night of the performance, we had Ike on bass guitar and my backup singers on their group microphones. I was out front in green tights and a retro looking wrap dress. Oh, and a wig. I can't forget about the wig! I lip-synced, we danced and had the crowd rocking with us. It was so nice they asked us to perform it the following day for the entire school. It was great!

This year, I had planned to perform a choreographed routine that my sister had put together. Something closer to this decade, upbeat and fun. With all the drama and chaos, I'm so over this school year. I'm ready for it to roll on past me. The foolishness, buffoonery, lies and cover-ups have taken too much of my energy, too much of my time and I just don't want to be a part of this anymore.

On this day, in hell, I'm included on a deceitful email in which the Lead Teacher for Special Education stated that she didn't see the Spawn of Satan kick me, but rather saw the student kick "at" me. She further mentioned that it seemed as if I had "everything under control." I'm wondering how she came to this conclusion when I asked for help repeatedly. She also stated that my door was closed. That's another lie. Let me ask reasonable people this-how would I have closed my door behind me when I am lifting a child in an attempt to remove them from the classroom? So another lie.

What we are faced with are a lot of people who don't want to do their job. People who want to cover up the issues so they can protect the people with whom they rub shoulders with. The same people who can put their hands on a teacher and be in the building the next school day. Wow! But if any one of us put our hands on another adult (let alone a child) we would be at a standoff with the entire state of Georgia's SWAT team.

The regional superintendent, she has to go! She has sat on her ass and protected this cow, year after year after year. She has got to go. She is the person who is blocking the superintendent from knowing what's going on in this school. She has got to go. Anyone that can sit back and allow the school (and several in their jurisdiction) to crumble—they have got to be removed, they are not for the educating of our children.

These systems are crumbling because people have truly forgotten how to care. There is no compassion in these poor parts. It's all about a check, retirement and benefits. Stop voting for these people, these so-called "*leaders,*" and then forget to hold them accountable to their platform. These parents need to stop having babies, forgetting that their wellbeing, growth and development is still their utmost responsibility. You cannot just have a baby and leave it up to these weak systems to educate your child. This is why they are failing! How can a teacher, who is in the trenches of hell…give their all, when their all is constantly attacked?

As a parent, there is no legitimate reason why you are sending me a letter three days before the end of the school year asking for your child to be tutored. Where were you the entire school year? Where were you when I asked you to help me with your child's disruptive behaviors? At this point, I have nothing else to give your child, not even a summer packet. How is it that your child is in my class not knowing the alphabet, letter sounds or even sight words? Why haven't you shown up?

This. This place. This system. This thing called "education." This isn't it. This isn't learning. This isn't teaching. This is babysitting. This is the penal system expressed in their lives at an early age. This is corruption. This is failure. This. This is not it!

Day 103:

Two meetings were scheduled with guardians without my prior knowledge and consideration for my schedule. Had they inquired prior to setting up a meeting, they would know that I had a previously scheduled doctor's appointment that I very much intend to be on time for. So needless to say, I was not present.

One of the meetings were prompted when a parent, three days before school is out, wonders why their child is failing. Um, sir, your child is failing because he never does homework, he rarely sits in his seat to receive instruction, he doesn't know letter sounds, may know two pre-primer (pre-kindergarten) sight words despite having interventions that allow him to be in a small group for at least 20 minutes a day. You, sir, have failed your son and have failed to follow through with my suggestions and requests for assistance. Now you and the school counselor can figure out what's the next step because I have checked all the way out.

The other meeting was prompted because the wild student, the Spawn of Satan, kicked me in my left leg and now there is a massive cover up and fear that I will call the police. In my absence, I'm told that the confused stringy haired girl never acknowledged that the wild satanic child is a nuisance. It was alleged that the only issues that the student has, derive from my classroom. No mention that this same confused teacher has had her glasses deliberately broken, has been hit by this same student and has had her classroom destroyed by this same student. Nope, it was all just something I created in my mind. Really?

They can have their stupid ass meetings and this school can remain in hell. It's too much bullshit and refusal to "call a thing, a thing." We will never get the help we need. No one wants to help.

They would rather allow this place to go up in flames. Students continue to suffer academically. Instead of correcting the issue, the school system would rather allow a worthless, compassionless principal to retire with full benefits. A shame! And her supervisor will continue to cover it up because she is knee deep in shit and I'm sure if they start sweeping from under the rug they will have her job as well. Pathetic!!!

Day 104:

I'm looking around my full classroom wondering why they are still coming. Sad, but true! Stay home, start the summer off early. Grades have been submitted, no more grading assignments for me. There will be no end of the year party. So, what are you holding out for? Stay home!

Day 105:

The last day of school was what, sweet. Nothing bitter about it. I'm ready, you all are ready, let's just get on with it. I have no cause to look back, no goodbyes to say. I'm just all the way over it. As far as I am concerned, consider me retired from this so-called field of education. This is not at all what I signed up for. Over it.

"...this really shed some light on my last year of teaching. I left the classroom after teaching for 13 years. #1 I was truly done with it all. I don't have to explain because you all already know what it is. #2 I wanted to pursue my goal of becoming a School Counselor. I'm in school now and the chapter I was reading about was on stress. I took this test based on how I felt last year. OMG!! Let me just say my numbers were RIDICULOUSLY high. I didn't even realize I was that stressed. Who knows where I would be now if I hadn't left. I've seen

several posts about educators being frustrated with their current situation. Please consider your health first! If there's a problem, do what you can to change it. Change schools, positions, careers, etc. You're no good to anyone if you're in the hospital. It's not worth it. Hopefully this helps someone." ~L.E. (Georgia)

However long the night, the dawn will break. ~ African proverb

Chapter 3: Ineffective Leadership Is Why We Leave…I Said It

"Principal: Good Morning! I'm bringing you a new student! Let's welcome him!

You (Teacher): Is he ok?

Parent: Oh, the other previous schools (10), that he has attended in the last 8 weeks, just don't understand him! He's really a good kid that needs LOTS of SUPPORT!

Principal: We are NOT here to SUSPEND students, but rather, give them ALL the SUPPORT they need!

You (Teacher): Ok! Welcome! What's your name?

Student: Your daddy's name, punk!

You (Teacher): What did you say?

Principal: (whispers in teacher's ear): We get $7,000 per student! Make it work!

Parent: Have a good day son!

Student: I hate you mom!

Teacher: I need to find a new career! (Thinking to [myself])."

~T.K. (Detroit, Michigan)

What is the leader of the schools' (i.e. "Principal") role in maintaining a level of balance within the school? With balance, I mean—teachers who desire to remain at the school, ideal work conditions (such as a workplace free from hostility, a safe environment), the opportunity to teach. Plenty of research has shown that the teacher directly affects the student and the teacher is one of the key components in student achievement. After all, the teacher is the first person held accountable when the student DOES NOT achieve. Yet, it seems that the teacher's environment is not taken into consideration.

Teachers are held accountable even before the parents are held accountable. If the child fails, it's the teachers fault. If the child cannot read, yet tons of interventions were done, it's the teachers fault. Paperwork that comes along with the students who require interventions are another way to micromanage what one is doing in the classroom. If the child is misbehaving in class, it's the teachers fault. Unlike the parents, teachers are held accountable for everything that goes on inside and outside of the class room. Again, what about the parent?

Could this be because no one is paying attention? I'm sure. Coming from a school with the turnover rate being as high as it was, yet the "leader" was not put in a position of accountability? It's unclear as to why. Of course, we can all speculate. When will the real questions be asked to the appropriate people and when will those answers be expected? There are so many questions.

This "principal" was a problem before I arrived on the scene. So much so, that much of the staff was new. The chaos was rampant and clear instructions were rarely provided. It was as if the blind was leading the blind. And this was the norm.

Significant research has been dedicated to understanding the conditions for which teachers must do their jobs. In looking at the research, one particular dissertation which focused on Georgia schools, I found that many of the areas in which the researcher outlined is much of the reason why the school (under said leadership)...failed! The areas that were highlighted, were that of resources, time, support, leadership, and teacher empowerment (i.e. factors that contribute to positive working conditions). When broken down in this manner it was clear to me that we didn't have this. All of these factors were said to be what a teacher needs in order to affect student achievement. No wonder our school was failing across the board.

Where are the "Title-1[6]" funds? What is going on with the budget? Shouldn't there be "school improvement" funds or even meeting notes that shows where the allocation of this money is going? Where are the grant funds? I do recall the school having access to a yoga instructor (which I am all for) but what about funds being used to incentivize appropriately modeled behavior and encourage the strengthening of the students' academics. This place was completely out of control.

It's not quite rocket science. It's a level of care and concern that one must have in order to effectively seek out the cause and rectify it immediately. Care and concern of which it seems this districts school board doesn't have. Probationary accreditation status, nepotism and the hiring of family and friends, indictments of former Superintendents (with charges of racketeering, bribery and

---

[6] According to the Department of Education, "Title I, Part A (Title I) of the Elementary and Secondary Education Act, as amended (ESEA) provides financial assistance to local educational agencies (LEAs) and schools with high numbers or high percentages of children from low-income families to help ensure that all children meet challenging state academic standards".

theft by taking), school shooting and hostage situations—who can keep up? Consumed with the scandals that plagued the county and shed light on corruption, again, it's no wonder those in the trenches get looked over.

No one stops to think of how this is affecting our children, nor is there a moment to stop a see how this is affecting our schools. Again, shit rolls downhill. So the shit that plagues the county also plagues the schools and those who are elected to "leadership" positions. It doesn't stop there. It trickles right into the classroom, on the backs of teachers and ultimately affects how we, as teachers, interact with the consumer (the student).

Add to this, a lazy principal who is more concerned with retirement and being messy-and a hostile environment is created. Only for so long can you push an adult human being in a corner and expect them to cower. Soon, teachers either leave, transfer or are forced out. I didn't do either, although at times I wanted to. This task was way bigger than the principal's waistline and way bigger than what I thought of my purpose.

What affects teachers working conditions, you ask? Let us first dig into the resources, which includes the building in which one works. We need supplies. That's simple, right? One would think so. Teachers send out a school supply list, asking parents to purchase as much as they can to facilitate in the classroom instruction. The problem, sometimes, is the priority a family places on said supplies.

Many in the education arena can attest to watching children come in with one hundred dollar sneakers and not have a pencil to complete their lessons. These are the "priorities" in which I speak of. This has been my experience. Now, this isn't every parent or family. Some families simply do not have the finances to keep up with the demand of what's often needed. That's typical within some "Title-1" schools. It's just the culture of that environment.

Lastly, looking to the school for supplies can be an arduous task. A lot of times, more often than one thinks, we (teachers) spend money from our own paychecks to create or purchase the supplies needed. Yes, "Title-1" funds are allotted for certain materials but that doesn't always make it to the classroom. My guess, look in those locked closets and see why.

This particular school had STEM equipment locked away in a "storage" closet. I know this because I saw it and inquired about it. I was very open and excited (even volunteering) to assist in running the STEM program. That chance never happened. Of course, I learned a lot of the reasons why. The "leader" of the school, and remember I use this term so very loosely, creates such a hostile environment that one can hardly stand to be there beyond the contractually obligated time. Long story short, in my three years at this HELLementary school, no STEM program.

If resources are handled properly (provided and made assessable), can schools thrive and even soar to achievement? Possibly. It's worth a shot in trying. Close one gap and continue to remedy the others. Trying is better than not.

The schools themselves need an overhaul to ensure the upkeep. Think about how cluttered and dirty environments affect the moods, attitudes and behaviors of a person. To think children are unaffected would be absurd. How can a child thrive in a disheveled environment? Granted, we had an awesome custodial staff, but it wasn't enough. Due to disruptive behaviors (which I will definitely get to), an antiquated building structure-the school maintained a lingering smell. The bathrooms were notorious for smelling like the inside of a pigs' colon.

Until we had new lights installed throughout the building, everything was glum. Truthfully, with the installation of the lights, we could now notice the asylum colored walls. Still there was sullen energy that encompassed the place, it just so happened we could see down the halls. What we saw, were buckets that collected water. Not just when it rained, but often enough that it became the norm.

But why weren't parents or anyone saying anything? Parents attend awards ceremonies and must maneuver through chairs placed over puddles as if they were caution signs. There were the constant buckets and trash bins that sat under oversaturated, murky brown acoustic ceiling tiles. Oh, but let us not speak on the wood planks with nails sitting on the playground (for over a month). That would just be bizarre.

Is it about politics? It absolutely is. The schools and parents on the Northside of town would never hear of such a thing. As pearls are clutched, there would be an uproar and an outrage. Why then, in our areas, are we not afforded the same? Dare we mention class or even race?

What's good for one area, should be good for all. Again, we are talking about the effects of student achievement. The environment absolutely contributes to that. The environment contributes to teacher satisfaction as well.

One area that helps us teachers is access to quality professional developments. Because our school was so low (failing), it seemed that everything was made into a "professional development." We met every week for the scheduled afterschool staff meeting. Because we were targeted as a failing school, with the idea that the school would be taken over by the State, we "met" every day during planning periods.

You might wonder what these meetings were about, since we were meeting so much. In all actuality, the meetings were a bunch of fluff that would be added to the "school improvement" notes. The meetings were a way to document that we were having a meeting and attempting to be on the same page. What these meetings were, in all actuality, were a sounding board for the inept principal to use as a platform to tell us what we weren't doing right. It wasn't professional development or shared decision making. Not at all. It was kicking us when we were already down. Communication (a meeting of the minds), the way I see it, is a mutually earned and invested component of a relationship. One must listen and hear. She chose not to listen or hear us.

The meetings during our planning periods (i.e. teacher collaboration), were typically unscheduled, but scheduled. We were told that it was daily, but there would be times when the "instructional coach" didn't show up. What it looked like was an attempt to say that we are being assisted by our instructional coach. And by instructional coach, I mean a friend of the principal who was not qualified to be an instructional coach. She didn't know her ass from her tennis ball head. Now granted, she may have been great as a special needs teacher, but the transition of her being the "instructional coach" was a reward for her new position as best friend forever (i.e. BFF). Anyone who had eyes could see it. She was groomed and put in position to be a "yes" person.

Our planning periods were typically spent listening to the principals' yes person ramble and fast talk the issues which would often be repeated in the next meeting. It became too much. Not only was she taking away our precious planning time, but we had plenty of work to do, papers to grade, copies to run off and calls to parents to make. But again, we were meeting to appease a status quo. So, time, is a valuable commodity that teachers need in order to be effective.

Because we were pushed, shoved and corralled into dysfunction, it gives the impression that our time and ability to prepare was often wasted. The show must go on. So if I cannot get it done at school then it must go home, which takes time away from my own family. That, to me, is a lack of consideration. Improper planning on the "leadership" part meant my day was ultimately rerouted. That is, if the expectation is to meet the needs of the children.

Things changed a lot, all the time and last minute. Notices to go home would be sent, expecting parents to read the document as soon as the child came home and get to the school for an event, meeting or conference the same day. For me, it begs the question, do you want the parents to participate, or don't you? The district had a portal in place where parents could see the students' grades, yet parents consistently didn't have access to the portal and tech support was hard to come by. Given the condition of the school, by "leadership," parent participation wasn't desired.

Not having the support or a parent's ear means a teacher is left unempowered. Without the direct communication with the parents anything goes. With all things rolling down hill, if we don't have the ear of the parent, the children are left to their own devises. Student discipline is affected and becomes a factor within the classroom.

Clear plans and strategies should be in place for the discipline of the students within the school. We didn't have that. We had one full time disciplinarian, in a leadership position, whose hands were tied when it came to carrying out the discipline needed for the school. When a disciplinarian was hired and extremely effective, we found that the position was quickly outsourced. So, the right question would be to ask this "leader" if they actually wanted change. I'd say she didn't-because she thrived in hellish environments. And we clearly were in hell.

One way in which a leader can be effective is by being visible. Not simply standing in the hall at the beginning of the day to intimidate teachers—but be visible in the sense that one is supporting instruction, discipline and management of the overall school. The buck was always passed. This "principal" refused to handle anything that fell in her lap and chose to send it to someone else. Often, this meant things didn't get done in a timely manner because those who actually work are doing other needed jobs. The "principal" would hide out, in rooms that became her second office, from parents and the needs of teachers/staff.

Being visible is walking your campus to see and ensure that it is safe as well as aesthetically appealing to the eye. When it rains, the school floods. Students would have to jump puddles to get from their classroom to certain "specials." The garden area, unkempt. The grass would grow close to one's knees before it would be cut and then the job was shabbily done. I can't recall ever seeing the grass edged up by the sidewalks. One year, I volunteered to take a gardening course to assist with school beautification. Needless to say, the paperwork was not returned and I missed the deadline. I was willing to assist in making the school beautiful. In my opinion, it's easier to maintain a thing rather than do a complete renewal (which is what was needed). Not only would this assist in making the school beautiful, but also give students an opportunity to learn how to manage the upkeep and take pride in their school.

The discipline problem was so bad within the school, across the board, that substitute teachers wouldn't accept the jobs. This lead to an influx and frequency of teachers trying to hold down an absent teacher's classes. Often it was the special area teachers who had to "substitute." In turn, this affects one's specials (i.e. planning time). It also may add additional children in the classroom. The behaviors were consistently out of control and I'm not speaking on a lack of classroom management, because veteran teachers were going through hell maintaining support from majority of the administration. We simply did not have the support of an effective schoolwide discipline plan.

I remember bringing it to the attention of "leadership" that I felt slighted when a child that has been removed from my class was allowed to play computer games after just being in trouble. This is pretty clear to me that we seem to reward bad behaviors. After certain instances, these children would look to misbehave in order to go with the "instructional coach" who was notorious for allowing the children, who behaved this way, to receive a "reward." This is not how teams operate. How can we be on the same team when we are pitted one against the other?

New teachers have come in with unapproachable demeanors, a reluctance to speak or even communicate with the teachers who had been there at least a year. Enough teachers experienced it to where it became a conversation and an acknowledgement. This particular year, the "principal" went to a hiring fair-taking her flunkies (fake instructional coach and fake technology teacher but not the assistant principal).

It was only later, after the teachers began to see the dysfunction, that we would find out that the teachers were "forewarned" about "troublemaking" teachers. I took this as an opportunity to learn more, in which I found out that the "principal" would hire the teachers but make comments about other teachers while in the interview process. I'm telling you, this "lady" thrived in drama. The "principal" would tell the new teachers to stay away from certain teachers and that she was trying to "clean house". What's the motivation for telling a new person anything of the sort, even if it were true. Which it wasn't.

Her goal may have been to keep division or keep certain people close to her. I mean, that was the only way in which you would be shielded from her wrath. Of course, you had to kiss a lot of ass but you wouldn't be bothered. Some people took that position and wore it well. They were handsomely rewarded for their efforts. Lush positions that one didn't have the credentials for, out of state "professional developments" and the friendship of the one who is a friend to none.

So, leadership is a thing of question. Does leadership affect student achievement and work conditions? Sure thing. If the leader isn't really a leader but a bully, what does it do to the mentality of the one who is being bullied?

Lack of leadership creates division and I've clearly shown true examples of such. Strong leadership equals strong schools, poor leadership equals a poor school. We encompassed all of the makings of a poor school and poor leadership. There was no trust. There was no support.

The turnover rate, supports that this person was difficult to work with. There had been incidents of children abusing teachers and no help for the teacher. There were situations where teachers were alleged to have said something inappropriate to a student (as in my situation), teachers alleged to have hit students (as was the case of several of my colleagues) and at least one incident where the principal grabbed a teacher (leaving her with a bruise). These situations are not isolated. These situations happened because we, the few, stood for something and couldn't sit back to allow the school (our students) and our morale to suffer.

In these incidents, the principal looked out only for herself. Possibly hoping to be a hero or attempt to bring justification of how she viewed us teachers, her staff, as incompetent. A teacher could come to work, expecting to do their job and within the next moment have a police officer surrounding her with questions of alleged abuse to a child. She has done this. It has happened! Ask those teachers.

I'm aware of a teacher who was cornered and asked to make copies of falsified documents for The Cow. Of course this teacher, at the time, didn't know what she was making copies of. She later found out that The Cow was building a case against another teacher and other "administrators" within the building with written statements to support the lies. The targeted teacher was warned and even presented with an attorney that showed her how, why and where they made a mistake. Unfortunately, it seems that the teacher that was targeted, didn't fight back and later transferred to another school. What happened, often, is that the teachers were found to have not hurt or said anything to a student and because of the hostile environment and distrust of The Cow and her minions, the teacher simply elects to leave for another school.

Leadership is being an advocate for the teachers. Not only do we lose teachers to the distrust, but also to the shuffling and reassigning of grade levels. It happens-this is understood but where is the advocacy to ensure mastery (utilizing a teachers' strengths)? The changing of important documents, such as lesson plans, in January is to benefit whom exactly? Assistance with these lesson plans didn't come from the "instructional coach" as she simply repeated and then restated what she already shared with us and ultimately YouTube videos sent as a teaching modality. A lesson plan is but one tool, yet so much emphasis was put on this 15-page document without the proper structure to assist with a conceptual understanding.

Leadership should involve a level of incentives and acknowledgement. Oh, wait, we had that at one time. At some place in time we had an opportunity to earn recognition for the works being done in the classroom and with the students. Just like most things in this school, there was a lack of consistency from the way in which the incentive would be earned and given out. One year, I earned a ticket for receiving my children early from their lunch break (which I didn't have an issue with in the first place) but my teammate was early and she reported that she didn't get a ticket. It didn't matter because I was never given the opportunity to know what the ticket would be used for or how it enhanced what I was already doing. Opportunities for a better school environment would begin and then slowly fizzle out with little mention of it.

These same teachers that I have had the pleasure of working with, have gone on to receive special awards in education (teacher of the month/year etc.), completion of dissertations, movement into leadership positions in other counties/districts, launching of businesses and simply thrived after the madness that once overwhelmed them. With all of these great accomplishments, we can't all be horribly, unskilled, indolent educators. We earned our degrees. We know our craft. We chose this life, but not this treatment.

All in all, ineffective leadership and atrocious working conditions drive great educators away, in droves. If there is a high-level of attrition-ask yourself why. If that doesn't settle you, ask the teacher or several teachers. Ask the regional superintendent, ask the superintendent. Go to the meetings and ask them. The answers might be closer than you think. While this is all very simple and easy to understand-the district continues to snub educators and parents. Even when it was in their face. There is no honor amongst thieves.

If all of these aren't reason as to why a teacher would leave a school (let alone the field), let's consider the average income of teachers. According to the National Center for Educational Statistics (NCES), the national average of a teacher's salary is between $42k-$52k. Of course this average can fluctuate between states, certifications and degrees. It's a decent wage, considering we affect the lives of so many and provide the bridge to every other career path in the world.

Now the research that I read spoke on using certain information (such as the school's website, school improvement notes, planning notes, budget and visits to the school) to help correlate teachers job satisfaction as well as the type of condition the school was in. If we were to consider this particular school, under said "leadership," what would we find? Much of it, I'm sure, would be fraudulent. How could it be precise and still allowed to function as it has under said leadership for such a length of time.

Why, again, in this day and age are we having budget cuts in education? How? How is there no funding (or a lack of funding)? It seems to me like the 4-11 thousand dollars that a district gets for each student, each year (which doesn't include the higher funding for children in special needs) should be considered when passed out to all these degrees sitting on their asses. Follow the funds, you find the corruption.

"DeKalb County teachers in Title One and Horizon schools are suffering because the top people in the district are not ensuring that principals put the right processes in place to help all teachers be effective in the classroom (another certified competent teacher). Response to Intervention [RTI] is a raggedy process that impacts teachers and students negatively because the county should hire teachers to do RTI by pulling these extremely low [scoring] children. Teachers and students suffer when turnover rates are massive because it's expensive and impossible to replace proficiently experienced teachers, and such was the case at [the school I left]! Principals should not be allowed to have all the power; that's a problem in many [county] Schools. In the spirit of SAVE THE TEACHERS, M.L.W." (Georgia)

A leader who does not take advice is not a leader. ~ Kenyan proverb

Chapter 4: A Call To Action

Parents

I challenge you to see what is going on in your child's school and begin to care. You can show your support by attending the parent teacher conferences and being available for the Parent Teacher Association (PTA) meetings. Join. You are needed.

Get to know your teachers and see what their needs are. You would be surprised how you can assist and volunteer even if its allowing the teacher to send home laminated documents for you to cut for the classroom. When you become involved, you see and understand the changes that take place within the school. You are the first to know.

Being a part of your child's academic career serves several different purposes. It shows your child that you care about their education and their future. It also puts you in a position to speak up on the needs of your child, their classroom and the school body as a whole. Parents, you hold the keys to a successful school year.

In my experience, with just this particular school year, some parents overlooked this vital component. No matter how many days they walked the halls of the school, many never spoke up to the atrocities that they witnessed or heard about. Some parents would walk right past the buckets lining the hallways with stale water from the dilapidated roof. Parents have seen the dangerous construction scraps left on the playground, leaving their children victim to unnecessary accidents. How could this happen?

Teachers/Colleagues

"When I have stressful moments and want to give up...these memories keep me pushing. [Third] Graders at [my elementary school]... Cried our last day of school last year because I was leaving the district. They were [a] mess but I broke down even worse after those buses pulled off. Memories like these are what makes you realize the reason behind teaching. The impact I made on these babies are the impact that I strive to make on every child I encounter." ~T.L. (South Carolina)

All too often, the teachers that are going through hell at the hands of administration are flouted. I understand. Sometimes you don't want to be involved. But what I learned, not getting involved is the very fuel by which these bullies thrive.

Think about the children we serve. When they are bullied, many times their "victims" operate from a position of lurking in the shadows, hiding their abuse. This is no different in how certain administrators hide behind their devious smiles yet unfairly evaluate the "victim" who begins to stand up for him or herself. And they do so with your support.

When we don't speak up for that teacher, standing side by side with these teachers, we give permission for the abuse to continue. Yes, it is abuse. I have seen great teachers leave the field or go to other schools to avoid the perceived wrath of an unhappy administrator who was skillful at poorly evaluating the people she bullied. Teachers, my colleagues, great teachers have been cornered and left to fend for themselves with false allegations. I knew about it-but I didn't know how to help them. We have a moral responsibility to address the abuse that we are aware of, and to do something so that it does not continue.

From this point on, not knowing is no excuse. We must stand together, supporting ourselves, supporting our children, upholding proper education. Why else were we drawn to this field? We advocate—that's what we do. Not only for the children but for ourselves too. When we unify, things will change.

Principals

"Such a shame how SLOW they [the school system and administrators] move to address the safety of children but FAST for their own safety. If I only made a few phone calls and quietly worked for a solution for my son…I would never have known how blatantly apathetic some administrators and school systems could be. Private or public teaching and administrating can wear you out, I'm sure. I am neither. Our children, my son, cannot reverse what happens to them. So as SOON as you get so tired, you ignore the critical needs and safety of our children, change professions quickly please. Keep people around you that will tell you the truth about what is unacceptable about your behavior and apathy in regards to our children." ~Anana Harris Parris (Mother and founder of the Sister Care Alliance)

I've had the amazing pleasure to work alongside awesome administrators. I remember working in a school in Maryland where the principal and assistant principal were one. They supported one another. This school was awesome. It wasn't without its own challenges, but there was peace, order, structure and learning taking place.

When the assistant principal isn't supported by the principal, run! When the principal isn't supported by the assistant principal, run! If there is no unity amongst the leaders of the school, then it's quite likely that there will be very little support for the teachers. As they say, "shit rolls downhill." If they can't work through their differences then it's probably not going to be very much room for you to teach, learn and grow.

Think about it in the context of a marriage/family. If the head of the household says yes, and the next in command says no, where does that leave you? Probably fighting to have your voice heard. Maybe left to your own devises. Either way, who is looking out for the most essential resource—the student?

In my humble opinion, a principal should be secure enough in herself that she can accommodate the needs of the teachers which essentially benefits the children of her school. A principal should have a level of leadership to where she can demand a level of respect—not to be confused with fear. A principal should have integrity, passion and concern. She should have people in her corner that have earned their position and aren't afraid to respectfully disagree (in fear that their "position" will be lost). These are the things I admire most in principals and assistant principals.

Principals, look at your iron fist and see if it's truly necessary. Ask yourself what are you afraid of? Deep down inside, are you a teacher who is ready and willing to assist your colleagues? Are you honest and genuine in the things that you do? Consider your turnover rate-do people want to stick around or get far away from you? These things are important to assess. You have a lot of work to do. The children are counting on you, or someone like you to lead them into victory. Is your school failing? Maybe it's time to do some self-assessing.

"At times, our actions fall short of offering guidance and support to our children when we allow six-figure salaries to cloud our judgement". (Middle School Parent, Maryland)

Superintendents

"I hope the time that the "one size fits all" logic in education ends before I retire. I just hate how they compare kids test scores, teaching strategies, etc. when you are dealing with different kids, parents, economics, etc. within a school, district, the nation, or worldwide. Apples to oranges every time." ~K.F.

You have got to get in these schools. Sitting behind your fancy desks and allowing your representatives to parrot back to you isn't working. Someone is lying and you should figure out who.

If you are my colleague, you are in the trenches with me. You help us get to the "promised land" come hell or high water. We have been suffering too long—drowning in political bullshit. When does it stop? This county is suffering through the loss of unethical practices, loss of accreditation and even financial fraud. When are you all going to clean this up?

Our children are looking at your smiling faces, which carry plenty of lies. What are you all here for? Are you here for the children or are your degrees and failed nepotism policy the foot that holds the door open for you? Us true educators are tired! We need help and you have failed us. Over and over again, failed us.

All sorts of mandates come down the pipeline. I don't deny that some of you are professional and scholars at research, but what I can't understand is how all these policies that affect the classroom continue to plague the classrooms at the same time. When is someone going to say, "Look, I really don't know what's going on in the classrooms these days, let me go check it out, see for myself. Let me speak to those that do know. Let me sit in a classroom." I'm not speaking about the classroom on the Northside, either. I'm speaking on the classes in the disenfranchised parts of town. I'm thinking about the areas that are saturated with "Title-1" funds. I'm encouraging awareness for the areas where the people come from destitute circumstances, the areas where people are often forgotten and hope is sometimes lost. I'm advocating for those who aren't sure how to advocate for themselves.

We know that you all talk, meet up for lunch and attend the same religious institutions, affiliated through your Greek letter fraternities and sororities—but let's talk about that which matters. With this ease of availability and comradery you share, speak about how you can support the teacher and in essence support the students. A lot of times it seemed as if the right hand (school board, superintendent and regional superintendent) didn't know what the left hand (The Cow and her failing school) was doing. Quite sad.

Until you, and your colleagues can begin to roll up your sleeves and jump in the trenches-many of you don't deserve the positions that you are currently encircling. Keeping those who would really make a difference, out of those positions are just as bad. If your children cannot thrive in the very schools that are suffering, then you sir/madam are not doing your job.

Chapter 5: Who Is Doing The Bidding?

"WOW! All I can say is WOW! Tom Bleakley is an attorney that represented the Detroit Public School board. I've had the opportunity to meet him and he was a fantastic legal representative. What he states [here] is how the DeVos family purchased the demise of Detroit Public Schools [DPS] to pave the way toward privatization of public schools and get their gal, Betsy, promoted to NDE by writing nice fat campaign contributions! Politicians are whores and will sell their asses to the highest bidders! Time to tell the elected officials they work for WE THE PEOPLE and we need to hold them accountable!!! The state of origin is Detroit, Michigan. Governor Snyder is the puppet of Dick DeVos. The DeVos family became rich from their Amway company which is seen by many as a pyramid scheme. They use their wealth to buy influence via campaign contributions on both sides of the isle thus allowing them to get their way when it come[s] to pushing privatization of public schools. Governor Snyder literally took 16 of our best schools building but the performance levels were low and created a new state run district called the Education Achievement Authority [EAA]

which was unsuccessful and those schools will be returned to the district next year 2017-2018. Something to note is that an audit has been requested over and over because those school buildings are attached to bond money and the EAA did not pay for the use of those building [thus] bilking DPS out of millions of dollars and the educational scores/status of those highjacked buildings did not improve." ~T.L. (Michigan)"

I now understand why unions are so very important. Having previously worked in an area where the school district operated and maintained a level of civility with respect to a teacher's union. I am all for holding people accountable through comradery and ethically establishing norms (and expectations) for a group of people. Operating in a school district, in a state where anything goes is absolutely absurd. Without the protection of a union, amongst a slew of savages, you get what you get and worse. And who is going to stop it?

Teachers buying into "protection" through memberships that claim to support teachers, but also protect principals (who by the way can also be members) is, or can be, potentially biased and cause a conflict of interest. I'm interested in knowing how many teachers have been bullied and harassed, sought help from the very system that protects the harasser, and actually received help! What sense does it make for the oppressed to seek help from those that protect or side with the oppressor? An abuser cannot help their victim until they first seek and accept their own help.

Whose interest is really being protected? Not to mention, in a "right to work[7]" state, also called "At-Will Employment" the mere questioning of "authority" puts one's career in jeopardy. This isn't

---

[7] Right To Work: *TITLE 34. LABOR AND INDUSTRIAL RELATIONS; CHAPTER 6. LABOR ORGANIZATIONS AND LABOR RELATIONS ARTICLE I. GENERAL PROVISIONS;* § 34-6-6. Compelling persons to join, or refrain from joining, labor organization, or to strike or refrain from striking. It shall be unlawful for any person, acting alone or in concert with one or more other persons, to compel or attempt to compel any person to join or refrain from joining any labor organization or to strike or refrain from striking against his will by any threatened or actual interference with his person, immediate family, or physical property or by any threatened or actual interference with the pursuit of lawful employment by such person or by his immediate family. (Enacted 1947.) (http://www.nrtw.org/right-to-work-states-georgia)

by design. It seems to me that the mob is very clear on how they intend to maintain "control" in these confederate minded states.

Throughout this journey, more often than not, several teachers have expressed going through similar situations, whether from a bully in leadership, harassing parents or even misguided youth who attempted to rule their classroom. Educators have lost their jobs, diligently sought other employment far from education, sacrificed their health and families for a career that painstakingly puts you at the caprice of tyrants on various levels. At this level, this is not what we signed up for. This is not what we spent years of advanced schooling and significant amounts of money to experience. In some ways, we simply wanted to change the world, one student at a time. Now, the face of education, is being changed through surreal policy, unrealistic expectations and lack of knowledge from those that make the decisions.

Chapter 6: Parents-Challenge and Change The System

"It's not enough to be right....be effectively right." ~C. Hassan Gale

Parents and family of children in schools, it's imperative that you remain visible, not only in the lives of your child but in their academic needs as well. You have no idea of the ways in which children and families are taken advantage of due to lack of parental knowledge of how things work and through your invisibility. Being involved essentially means being informed. One way to remain in the know, is to attend the Parent Teacher Conferences as well as join the Parent Teacher Association (PTA). Even then, this is not enough.

Each school district has board members. Know who they are. After all, your tax dollars contribute to their salaries. Attend the public budget hearings and see how the money is being allocated. Hold these members to what they say they will do.

The school board meetings allow you to listen to the decisions that are being made that will ultimately affect you and your family. During these discussions, your participation may be limited, however you can find out about the topics that are requiring a vote of the board. Often, your questions and concerns are addressed at the level of the teachers and administration and from there within the district level.

It's not enough to simply tell the principal but follow up with a formal email. Having worked under the "leadership" of a principal that circumvents responsibility (i.e. not effectively doing the job she is paid to do), it's important that you create a professional paper trail. Many times, a strong team is needed to ensure that appropriate action is taken.

Who is the team?

During my last year within the public school, I encountered pockets of parents who were actively engaged or sincerely concerned about the things they saw taking place within the school. Yet and still, there was little done to make things happen. This is because one voice, every so often, makes little noise. One angry parent is easily soothed and coddled into submission and silence. Then, ultimately, things go back to an asylum normal.

I also noticed that the Parent Teacher Association was strategically held at awkward times, with little to no notice. By design? Of course. This school knew that the power is with the parent. No parent equals no power and thus the lawlessness of a rogue principal.

The Parent Teacher Association is but one way in which to have a voice. I am of the sound mind that more than one association should be formed and joined. Understand the bylaws of the Parent Teacher Association, attend the meetings and be present-but be ready to move outside of the marionette strings of the system as a whole. Create your own association.

The first team should be structured of the parents. Pick a time and a place to have a meeting. Set an agenda to determine what you want to know, what you want to do and how you want to see it come into fruition. Again, all things need not be in place to get started. The main thing is an interest in your children succeeding within this system that isn't designed to see them succeed. The first meeting might be two people sitting at the dinner table with a simple desire.

As you begin to meet and are visible, you will attract other parents who have a similar idea and desire. Begin to establish guidelines by setting ground rules for your group. Restate the ground rules often so that it becomes the norm for your meetings and all who are in attendance are aware. By this time, you may want to have someone in the position of secretary or note taker. In this way, you can see the progress and keep a clear record of the goals and order of business.

Maintain a level of confidentiality early on. Speaking prematurely and to the wrong people can crush the momentum of any group. Some of the tasks that the group will work on should only be presented when all the information is ready. This same information should be presented in a professional manner and with unity of the group.

For instance, the group may have an idea or topic to present to the board. This topic should be thoroughly researched. Include in a letter to the school principal, the idea (problem and solution) and date in which you would like to discuss the information. This letter will have been written and presented to the group for approval and suggestions. This letter does not need to include each parents name or you may want to include the decided name of the group. Allow the principal a fair amount of time to respond. From the response, your group will know whether further action should be taken.

As a suggestion, communicate with the teachers their needs and ideas. There is often a thin line between the teacher and their employer. As a teacher, we often want the best for our children/students yet our hands seem bound quite often. The strength is in the parents voice. You are the first line of defense when it comes to your child.

Should you need to take your letter and interest to the school board, determine the meeting in which the group will attend. Bring as many of the members as possible. Ensure that this is a meeting in which the community can present information. Respectfully (and thoroughly) present your concerns.

The beauty of having a solid group is that there is strength in numbers, unity and thoroughness. Each member may not make every single district meeting, but someone from the group should be there so that the group is represented and has first-hand knowledge. To be effective, at the core level, you need passion. That passion should be fueled by knowing that your child deserves the best.

Chapter 7: Demands Must Be Met

"Who is doing the damage to this society? Men of power and intelligence and distinction who choose to build prisons and reject providing an opportunity to learn for every child are educated people. Officials who make policies that say, 'We must raise standards, we must extract a level of competency from children,' but feel uncomfortable about saying that we must first establish a level of competency for those who teach the children. Those who say, 'We must raise standards and everything will improve,' but do not say simultaneously, 'We must provide the material and the personal resources,' are very intelligent, powerful people." ~Dr. Adelaide Sanford ("Education: The Moral Imperative". This is a transcript of the keynote address)

The first step is identifying that there is an astounding need for educational reform and comprehensive support of instruction. As educators, we know what it looks like, we know what it feels like to be in a disruptive environment, unable to function optimally. We know when our students can achieve greater results with better resources, adequate support and parental involvement that not only supports the child but instruction as well. We also know, when our needs are not being met and the alarming data that supports which schools continually have increasing gaps.

As well, many of us know what we envision when we think, "thriving school," "inspiration," "the educated child," "student success," "effective leadership," "achievement," "educational excellence," and "lifelong learning." The issue is, "Are we actually receiving any of that," and if not, how can we attain it? It's not enough to simply have core beliefs and a mission, but to faithfully, consistently and accurately carry out those beliefs and stand firm on the mission is what is of the utmost importance. What is the mission of the school, the county, the district and the Nation? Understand what they have agreed to and hold them accountable on all levels. Of course, some areas may be slack, but what is put in place to get it back on track or to create it. If there is no plan, the mission and vision should be updated or re-created.

As a teacher, what is your mission and philosophy on educating students? Does this mission or philosophy change from year-to-year? Does it change based on the class and the demographics in which you teach? Should it be fluid and be adjusted based on what your school needs and what you are able to provide? Possibly.

In looking at some of the missions that districts and schools are charged with, I notice that the underlining goal is that of student achievement, as it should be. I've taken the liberty of looking into some of the visions and missions that stand out and dissecting it so that it makes sense and can be used as a tool for accountability. The previous school, the HELLementary in which these entries were about, had a vision and mission statement that was consistently not adhered to—from the top down. They were great words, yet the lack of action to carry out the vision and mission were missing.

To point out, the environment was not positive, safe or nurturing as the mission suggested. How could it be positive and safe when students ran the school and one administrator abrogates the other in an attempt to undermine? The mission further claimed to prepare children for a technologically advanced society. Again, how is this possible when technology rarely worked and the technology teacher was a displaced teacher, being shielded from the loss of a job due to allegedly harming a child? Much of the lessons in technology were by way of free online computer games. Not to mention, a lot of the technology resources were locked away in "storage." Add to this the motto, how are we advancing our community and preparing them for success when we haven't yet met the basics of what we say we are here for?

Given the county and its lack of structure and criminal activity, one cannot help but see that the model is created from the top down. Some might say, the apple doesn't fall too far from the tree. My grandmother would further add, "If you lie, then you will cheat. And if you cheat, you will steal. And if you steal, you will kill." Simple, right? Well, the foundation is that of liars, cheaters and thieves and the end result is the death of our students desire to grow and learn and the desire of great teachers to remain in this county and sometimes the field altogether.

Some of the "beliefs" of the county is said (written) to provide exceptional school and district leadership. Fail. Cultivate learners who are valued…and held accountable for their actions.

Fail. Embrace diversity. Fail. As well as create environments where educational excellence is the standard/norm. Fail. That principal, this place, didn't do any of this. When these things happened, it was because of the teachers love for their students-not because the "principal" fostered an environment to do so.

So what is the solution? Not only are we to hold our schools and districts accountable for what they say they "believe" and "envision" for the schools but ensure that it happens. If not, change the belief, motto or vision. Simple, right?

What do we want for our schools? What is it, as a teacher, that makes the school great? What makes it viable, where you want to stay at a school for more than one year? As a parent, what does one foresee when living in one particular neighborhood, for the sake of zoning and school assignment? What makes a parent choose paid private schools versus free public schools or even homeschooling?

As an educator and parent, we want and expect teachers who desire to teach effectively and utilize strong/rigorous curriculums with high expectations. We want to see you in your position, loving what you do and challenging the youth to reach high and excel. I am of the sound mind that a person wants to enjoy what they do, especially if they've dedicated years to cultivate the craft, spent thousands upon thousands of dollars to be educated and become an expert in the field. Most educators are there because they know they can change the future, they diligently work to do just that.

We (educators and parents) want proper technology and training to reflect the proper use of said technology. It is said and understood that some schools need more resources than others. In these parts, many of the children come from homes where they may not have access to consistent technology and proper training of said technology. As we advance in a "technological" society, it's imperative that our children be introduced to these skills and become masters of the craft. In doing so, we can begin to prepare them to be "college and career ready" or entrepreneurs within their own right.

As an educator, we want to embrace each student's potential and be able to do so individually. A parent wants to know the intricate details of what their child knows and how they can assist at home. Learning is not a one size fits all model. Educators need time and proper resources to be able to assist their students in the next phase of their learning. As educators, we are like our students' parents, spending so much time preparing and fostering their academic needs. Many educators do not want their name attached to an ill-prepared child. We work hard to ensure that each child is learning. So we want to ensure that children are learning and can be supported through the process.

Diversity is so important. We want to embrace diversity in thought, word and deed. Understanding the diverse needs of the children we serve is not only academic, but cultural and spiritual/religious as well. The previous school, the HELLementary in which these entries were about, reflected a strong Muslim population. Many of the Muslim students were from the continent of Africa. Rarely, if ever, did I see anything that was accommodated to their needs.

True, we don't pray in school and there are laws that govern that, however on the same token being surrounded by Christian (in name) teachers, that particular culture was always present (even amongst the most devilish of them). While I'm not speaking on proselytizing, its only right and fair that we acknowledge the whole or exempt it all. Yes, this means your Christmas party. No matter which way you slice it, it leans toward one particular religion as opposed to including them all. Considering the diversity of the whole, there should be education or an acknowledgement of it all as it pertains to the children in which the school services.

Parents expect a safe a respectful environment. Educators need and want a safe and respectful environment. Children flourish in a safe and respectful environment. So what's the problem? Through consistent and clear expectations, we can have it. As a team, as partners, when we effectively create this safe place, we can then effectively foster and encourage self-discipline. It starts at home, yet some children may not get it there. So we as educators and the leaders of these institutions must create a reliable way to relate to the children and promote proper discipline. Children expect to have a level of structure.

We want (and demand) fairness within the district. Leadership should exemplify accountability. Educators are held accountable to the scores (success and fail) of their students, so why then is leadership not held accountable for their support (nonexistent or otherwise)? In no way should those in which we answer to, be given a pass for their inadequacies. Too many times, the "principal" in which I worked for was shielded by her own supervisors and possibly those above her. I was not the first to have a war waged against me. Why was there no accountability? Why weren't things investigated and looked into, as it was suggested, year after year? The common denominator was this hellish person, every time. The lack of concern became the model that was reflected from the top down. Leaders don't care, educators can only care so much and ultimately the reflection is classrooms/students with a lack of care and concern; whether academically or behaviorally. Children are very receptive and they know what's going on, even when we think they don't.

We need the support of our communities. Yes, the communities in which we educate are now our communities. We are responsible. At some point, we need to be able to engage the community. The doors (our hearts) should be open to the community. I believe that the valuing of the people within the neighborhoods, of our students, helps to develop a sense of belonging. Yet, we don't know the people nor do we know our students. We want and need the communities to be engaged in the learning successes of our students, we want the community to also be accountable for student success. We desperately need the village and the village mentality.

I can recall several instances in which my fifth-grade class didn't bring in their homework or I couldn't connect with a parent in a timely manner. Yes, I was notorious for pulling up a student's address and stopping by their home after school for an impromptu parent meeting. I needed the parents to know that I am concerned and that I am here to assist in any way I can. True, it could have been dangerous (venturing into the unknown), yet I allowed my heart to guide me. Jumping on unruly school buses, riding into their neighborhoods and speaking to parents who might not receive me well could have been dangerous, I get that. But we also must let our parents know (in real time) what is taking place. Again, we must be about the community, our community. We are our student's village.

Not only do I (educator and parent) want to see this happen. I know that it can happen. There is no such thing as a perfect school but there is a great expectation for great leadership. When we can meet at the mind and have the common foundational goal of student success, anything and everything is possible. Students will succeed when we succeed.

A man who uses force is afraid of reasoning. ~Kenyan proverb

Chapter 8: What Is A Workplace Bully?

Often, we hear of the childhood bully and the perceived ideal of this person as being a child (or student) who is larger in size than some of the others. You might assume that the bully is the child that has some degree of difficulty in their home life or is not as sharp as their peers. Sometimes, the bully might be the student that's perceived to be the troublemaker or a bit more difficult to maintain their attention in certain situations. Well, what if you could understand that these are stereotypical views of what a bully might look like? What if you could fathom that adults too can be bullied?

First, one would need to understand the working definition of a bully. According to stopbullying.gov[8], "Bullying is unwanted, aggressive behavior among school aged children that involves a real or perceived power imbalance. The behavior is repeated, or has the potential to be repeated, over time. Bullying includes actions such as making threats, spreading rumors, attacking someone physically or

---

[8] www.stopbullying.gov is a government website managed by the U.S. Department of Health & Human Services (200 Independence Avenue, S.W. - Washington, D.C. 20201) StopBullying.gov provides information from various government agencies on what bullying is, what cyberbullying is, who is at risk, and how you can prevent and respond to bullying.

verbally, and excluding someone from a group on purpose." While this is a really great definition, it doesn't focus much on adults. In fact, a lot of resources specifically mention bullying in the context of children. Yet and still, many of these definitions can identify an adult as being the bully (and the recipient of being bullied) if one chooses to replace words such as child etc. with adult, employee or supervisor.

According to the Workplace Bullying Institute, "workplace bullying is repeated, health-harming mistreatment of one or more persons (the targets) by one or more perpetrators. It is abusive conduct that is threatening, humiliating, or intimidating, or work interference (sabotage) which prevents work from getting done, or verbal abuse, is driven by perpetrators' need to control the targeted individual(s)." As with any abuser that seeks to gain power through control and manipulation, bullies seek out targeted individuals deliberately and unleash their madness in a cunning and sometimes surreptitious manner. However covert, to those who are not on the receiving end, the bully inflicts emotional and psychological damage that is exposed and directed at their target. While bullying is real on all levels, and includes children, I will be using the word bully (bullying etc.) in the context of workplace bullying and its effects on those who are, or have been, abused and affected by such cowardly actions.

It's important to note that one cowardly incident is hardly ever considered "bullying." Yet and still, the bully must begin somewhere. Bullying is typically several incidences that consciously attempts to hurt the recipient (or victim). Those who choose to bully are considered to have personality flaws or characteristics that deem them to be opportunistic, powerful (as in ones' supervisor) and even competitive.

According to Tim Gould[9], Anton Hout classifies bullies into eight different personality types. According to Hout, the bullies are the "screaming Mimi," the "two-headed snake," "the constant critic," "the gatekeeper," "the guru," "the wannabe," "the attention seeker," and "the sociopath." For me, just hearing these terms raised the hair on my arms because I could readily identify with whom I

---

[9] Tim Gould (www.HRMorning.com) and Anton Hout, founder of OvercomeBullying.org . *"The 8 most common bully personalities"*, http://www.hrmorning.com/8-workplace-bully-personality-types/

had been dealing with. To further drive the point, the descriptions of each bully appeared to be spot on with what I experienced.

In short, the "screaming Mimi" is a bully who enjoys being feared. This person is easy to identify in that they are often noisy and hateful. Check and check. Most people knew The Cow as being sly and hateful however she seemed to relish in intimidating tactics and the responses to them (seeing people squirm).

The "two-headed snake" comes off as upright meanwhile attempts to destroy, to include attacking one's professional character and their integrity. A snake to say the least, she is the epitome of a slithering serpent. Hello? Does anyone recognize this? This cow lied on me, several times and in the presence of her supervisor. And while doing so, she had to acknowledge that I was a good educator, with no previous issues within the school. This is one of the reasons why her supervisor couldn't understand how we had gotten to that point. Well, to understand how, you must understand the why. The why is because she is a scheming bully.

Then, there is the "constant critic." This type of bully wants to single handedly destroy the victim's confidence, to the extent of altering documents in an attempt to sabotage. Was I not on a PDP?

Were my last evaluations false and after being met with resistance she changed them to reflect my competency (which had been proven for the previous two years)? Did she not do this to other staff as well? These were the same staff who began to push back after being shoved too hard.

I've met many of the next type of bully's, possibly not in the bullying capacity but there are a few of them in the capacity of my "favorite people" in the whole wide world (secretaries and cafeteria ladies). The "gatekeeper" is the one who will deny resources etc. The gatekeepers will attempt to prevent a person from being proficient in their tasks. The Cow was the large gatekeeper and she had minions to do her bidding. Title-1 resources locked in "storage closets" unavailable to the children who could benefit from the resources.

The next bully lacks emotional maturity and will not accept responsibility. This bully will act as if they are "above the rules." Yes, this is the "guru." The better name could be "asshole" or "childish," however I digress, "guru" it is. The Cow was surely a guru in this light. Always pointing fingers and striving to shut grown and professional colleagues down.

The "wannabe" is a bully that is opposed to the ideas of others and will intentionally look for flaws to block areas for change and growth. She rarely, if ever, owned up to the problems within the school, even when they were apparent. Instead, the fingers were always pointed at the teachers as if we don't have experience or are simply unprofessional. When met with the opportunity to make the school better, she would often sit in meetings as if she already knew or as if "our school" is already doing that. Not only would it be lies upon lies, it allowed the entire school to suffer. How does the saying go? "Pride cometh before the fall." And she fell hard.

The bully who seeks the approval of others is called the "attention seeker." When the approval is not met, the bully turns on the person. During which time, personal information about the victim is gained and used on them. Sounds familiar? Well, this is how teachers who have businesses and other endeavors outside of school, found their way in front internal affairs, the regional superintendent, the police and even the school board, defending their position to remain an educator.

Lastly, the bully that is intelligent, yet lacks empathy, is known as the "sociopath." How fitting! One cannot deny, she appears to know her stuff, yet her knowledge and scholarship is overshadowed by her manipulative ways. Not only is the psychopath-I mean, sociopath dangerous but she enlisted the help of others to do her dirty bidding. The minions fell victim to nepotism by way of wanting or needing a better position. They got sucked in and you know, once you dance with the devil-the devil changes you[10].

Based on these understandings of the bully, as powerfully expressed by Anton Hout, I would say that many of the characteristics showed up on any given day within my workplace. Not only were they visible, but they dangerously changed the environment, and at times the personalities, of people who simply wanted to make a difference in the lives of children. I certainly was changed, and affected. I became physically sick, emotionally tired, withdrawn, angry and near abusive.

Bullying can appear differently and show up in many ways, depending on the level of The Cowards professed authority, the recipient and the degree to which they are successful in getting away with the unwarranted acts. In some instances, bullying can be

[10] "If you dance with the devil, then you haven't got a clue, for you think you'll change the devil, but the devil changes you." - J.M. Smith

threats, manipulation, isolation, micromanaging, sabotaging one's efforts, rumors and even isolating the recipient.

Chapter 9: The Toxic Work Environment

Bullying affects everyone. It affects the recipient in ways that show up in one's health. A typically healthy individual may begin to exhibit and internalize the stress-related symptoms which begin to show up as high blood pressure, psychological attacks in the form of thoughts that are unhealthy (homicide, assault, vandalism), anxiety, depression, Post-Traumatic Stress Disorder and even suicide. A recipient of bullying and harassment may have a decreased desire to perform productively, which may show up in the lack of aspiration to be present at their job (i.e. tardiness and absenteeism). Bullying affects the overall work environment as other employees may witness the abuse yet be unable or unwilling to take action. This too can cause undue stress-just from being a bystander (or witness). Not only does it affect the business or company in which one works but it also affects the recipients home life. A parent may not have the added energy to parent, a spouse may not have the yearning to be present and available for their spouse. Personal relationships have the potential to become burdened and strained.

Physically, the effects of being bullied, in the workplace, may show up as many of the symptoms of stress. There may be a decrease in energy, frequent and unexplainable headaches, body aches, chest pains, sudden weight loss or weight gain. A person may experience a loss of hair, the inability to sleep (insomnia), a lack of sexual desire and even susceptibility to colds as the body begins to deteriorate under the pressure. These are all psychosomatic effects that take a toll on an individual that is being bullied. The effects of bullying are overpowering.

Emotionally, a person may find it difficult to relax in an otherwise safe and relaxing situation. The person may feel as if they are the ones losing control as they are having overwhelming thoughts. Some of these thoughts may bring about feelings of loneliness and low self-esteem. The person being bullied may become easily agitated or frustrated in different situations which can lead to avoidance of people that they typically would want to be around.

In the toxic environment, one might notice that there is a high turnover rate, as was the HELLementary in which the devil took her last dance. Not only was the turnover rate astronomically high (at least 20 new teachers my last year), but the morale was extremely low. Absenteeism then becomes an issue, as much needed breaks are frequent. It's difficult to maintain an efficient level of motivation when the levels of stress have attacked the body mentally and physically. Not only is bullying unhealthy, it costs the workplace money, time and resources. All of which cannot be missing in a school that's expected to assist the students in reaching academic achievement.

One who causes others misfortune also teaches them wisdom. ~ African proverb

Chapter 10: They Don't Really Care About Us

"Equal isn't always fair. Students report allegations against educators and they [educators] are removed immediately, allegations reported [on other personnel] within the system [get] slow reactions until something happens." A.R. (School Counselor, Maryland)

According to the United States Department of Labor[11] and the Occupational Safety and Health Administration (OSHA), "Nearly 2 million American workers report having been victims of workplace violence each year. Unfortunately, many more cases go unreported." These same agencies determine workplace violence to be "any act or threat of physical violence, harassment, intimidation, or other threatening disruptive behavior that occurs at the work site. It ranges from threats and verbal abuse to physical assaults and even homicide." So this IS a problem. Workplace violence and bullying isn't a new phenomenon, yet it happens and continues to happen on

[11] https://www.osha.gov/SLTC/workplaceviolence/

account of insecure individuals that are unable to maintain and balance authority in a healthy and productive manner.

There are laws that have been put in place to curtail abuse on the job. This information is required to be posted within ones' place of employment, however it may go unnoticed or even misunderstood. The Occupational Safety and Health Act of 1970 outlines duties and expectations. The Act, states its purpose, "To assure safe and healthful working conditions for working men and women; by authorizing enforcement of the standards developed under the Act; by assisting and encouraging the States in their efforts to assure safe and healthful working conditions; by providing for research, information, education, and training in the field of occupational safety and health; and for other purposes." Furthermore, in Section 5 under the heading "Duties," it further proposes, "(a) Each employer shall furnish to each of his employees' employment and a place of employment which are free from recognized hazards that are causing or are likely to cause death or serious physical harm to his employees; (29 USC 654) shall comply with occupational safety and health standards promulgated under this

Act. Each employee shall comply with occupational safety and health standards and all rules, regulations, and orders issued pursuant to this Act which are applicable to his own actions and conduct."

While I am no legal authority on the crafty words used in this realm of the law, I am clear that the assurance of safe and healthful working conditions implicitly means that I can expect to do my job without undue harm to my person. If a person, who happens to be in a supervisory position, is knowingly subjecting their staff to unsafe and unhealthy working conditions (whether mentally, physically or emotionally), this is against the law. Furthermore, the law states that the place of employment has a duty to have an accommodating place free from recognized hazards. I've recognized, as well as others have recognized and identified that the common thread of this place of employment was due to the menacing behaviors of someone in a position of authority. In which case, the unsafe environment created by the supervisor resulted in several incidents of employees (teachers) being hospitalized due to stress related incidents. And if memory serves me correct, stress leads to ailments that contribute to things that will likely cause death and serious physical harm. So why weren't we protected?

The Equal Employment Opportunity Commission (EEOC) defines harassment as, "unwelcome conduct that is based on race, color, religion, sex (including pregnancy), national origin, age (40 or older), disability or genetic information. Harassment becomes unlawful where 1) enduring the offensive conduct becomes a condition of continued employment, or 2) the conduct is severe or pervasive enough to create a work environment that a reasonable person would consider intimidating, hostile, or abusive. Anti-discrimination laws also prohibit harassment against individuals in retaliation for filing a discrimination charge, testifying, or participating in any way in an investigation, proceeding, or lawsuit under these laws; or opposing employment practices that they reasonably believe discriminate against individuals, in violation of these laws.[12]" Although the EEOC has laws protecting harassment, I am of the strong opinion that this law should include workplace bullying under the conditions that bullying crosses the lines of

---

[12] Equal Employment Opportunity Commission (EEOC) definition of harassment. https://www.eeoc.gov/laws/types/harassment.cfm

creating a “work environment that a reasonable person would consider intimidating, hostile, or abusive.” Whereas bullying may not always include some of the characteristics of harassment (based off race, religion, age, disability etc.), it most certainly can. If bullying cannot be added to this law, the EEOC should consider having a law against workplace bullying.

The EEOC further states that harassment can be the “victim’s supervisor” (similar to workplace bullying), and can include intimidation, threats and can interfere with one’s performance on their job (again, much like workplace bullying). While we know, and understand that prevention is key, this does not stop bullying (i.e. harassment) in the workplace from occurring. The definition of bullying, like harassment, should include steps to prevent it from happening, make others aware that it is happening, and limit the victim from retaliation once it has been reported. When these steps are not effectively in place, we experience it firsthand (whether personally involved or as a bystander, or third party), and it creates an environment where people may be apprehensive about coming forth and reporting the nature of bullying (i.e. harassment). Does the "whistleblower protection act" protect us in this case? Not hardly due to it following an "at-will employment doctrine."

As I have adamantly mentioned before, it is everyone's responsibility to ensure that bullying isn't happening and to report it when it does. Many times, the problem lies in the retaliation that one witnesses as the victim is currently at the receiving end of bullying abuse. Bullying creates an overall toxic environment.

According to the Workplace Bullying Institute[13] (2009), the Sioux City Community School District in Iowa, "is the first in the nation to launch an anti-bullying program with advocates trained to hear complaints from employees…[and are], partnering with the Waitt Institute for Violence Prevention in North Sioux City to provide training." If this program happened to address a problem, then why haven't other areas adopted such a program to address the statistically alarming problem that is being reported by the OSHA?

---

[13] " School District Program to Guard Against Workplace Bullying" by M. Sexton (September 18, 2009)

Chapter 11: Bullied? What Can You Do?

I suggest being vocal about what is taking place. Being vocal looks like different things to different people. One person might shout at the person who is bullying them whereas another person may speak to others about it. It really just depends on you and your personality and whether you are ready for the possible backlash governing the way in which you are vocal. You might simply let the person who is doing the bullying know that their behavior, words or intimidation is unwarranted. This acknowledgement and honoring of yourself might be enough to make the person refrain from targeting you any further.

If the person continues to harass and bully you, I would further suggest that you begin to keep a record of the incidents. Be as specific as possible, including dates, times and witnesses (if any). Be very clear on what constitutes harassment or intimidating behaviors. Some of the aggressors' behaviors may be clandestine (such as unscheduled meetings during your breaks or after work, it might be extra duties that are beyond your scope and even devious wording of your evaluations) and others may be obvious (rude comments, persistent lies and isolation). Detailed evidence will begin to paint the picture of the type of person you are dealing with. This documentation will show how often the harassment is occurring and show a pattern of the nature in which you are being bullied or harassed.

In dealing with a supervisor who is bullying you, understand that they cannot be trusted. Always keep records of the conversations being had. When possible, limit private conversations with the person. If a meeting is needed, seek out a respected mediator to be a witness of the exchange that takes place. Strive to do most of your interactions within the boundaries of an email. As with guileful bully supervisors, this is an area in which they will likely stray from. The last thing they want is to be on record as a harasser.

Understand the rules, regulations and policy governing workplace harassment and bullying. While there may not be much information on workplace bullying, thoroughly understand harassment in your workplace. Report the incidents as soon as possible and as often as possible. Many times, there are statues of limitations on reporting of any one incident. Should your concerns go unrequited, know and follow the chain of command. After a considerable amount of time has passed, and you feel that the actions are not being handled properly, it might be time to seek more radical approaches. Be sure that you are aware of the law in your area.

Of course, I am not saying that you should retaliate. While I do understand the psychology behind wanting to, it wouldn't be in your best interest and its quite possibly against the law. I had to talk myself off the ledge several times. I know and understand that I am not fit for an orange jumpsuit and plastic slides. So, the many times I thought about it, I decided against it.

Most employers have an Employee Assistance Program[14] (EAP) if you need to speak to someone. Speaking to someone about

---

[14] Employee Assistance Program, per the Office of Personnel Management (OPM), is a voluntary, confidential program that helps employees (including management) work through various life challenges that may adversely affect job performance, health, and personal well-being to optimize an organization's success. EAP services include assessments, counseling, and referrals for additional services to employees with personal and/or work-related concerns, such as stress, financial issues, legal issues, family problems, office conflicts, and alcohol and substance use disorders. EAPs also often work with management and supervisors providing advanced planning for situations, such as organizational changes, legal considerations, emergency planning, and response to unique traumatic events. https://www.opm.gov/policy-data-oversight/worklife/employee-assistance-programs/

your mental state, is not a sign of weakness. Often times, it was my speaking to someone that further helped me to step back from the ledge (so to speak). It was in these moments, that I realized how important it is to just speak about what's taking place, in an environment that is free from judgement. Granted, I paid for my own services, as I found the EAP through this particular county was limited and awful. My counseling sessions brought about great release, acknowledgement and suggestions that I hadn't considered. Also, it's another form of documentation of the hell that I endured under an oppressive regime.

If you are in a state of crisis, be honest with yourself. Seek help immediately. You are the most important factor in all of this. You being unwell benefits no one. Put yourself first and allow your support system to rally around you in your time of crisis.

Bullying is not an accident; it is done on purpose. Bullying occurs when one individual is perceived to have more power than another. There is a level of a power imbalance. Bullying is an abuse of one's authority. Bullying happens more than once.

The point is, we as educators have worked hard to acquire the necessary degrees and certificates to show ourselves approved within the field that we have chosen. We didn't chose this career to be bullied by principals, bullied by students, bullied by parents and/or be bullied by a system that closes their eyes to the needs of its children. When we, as educators, are pushed into a corner by the very "leaders" that are entrusted to be ethical, then we, professionals, can do one of two things. We can either become docile and play the game the way they want, which leads to destruction or we can fight for our lives, our passion, our students and for a just system that supports us and the children we serve. There is no other way.

An army of sheep led by a lion can defeat an army of lions led by a sheep. ~ Ghanaian proverb

Chapter 12: Building Yourself Back Up

As a working professional, it's often a thin and delicate balance in caring for others and caring for yourself. Know and understand that you are important and to be effective, you must be healthy (mind, body and spirit). Make time for your own self-care needs. If not for you, then who?

Some of the ways in which you can ensure that you are giving your body attention:

- Get fresh air daily. This is essential to your immune system, your digestion, your lungs and for clearing the mind.
- Movement (walk, run or bike). Many forms of exercise assist in strengthening your heart and reduces the risks of various diseases such as diabetes, plus exercise increases your energy.
- Set personal goals. Our goals propel us forward, keeping us focused and motivated.
- Participate in monthly massages. While in the midst of the chaos, I found that my body was in knots, constantly. The

massages helped me remember me and take a moment for myself.

- Read a great book. Keeping your mind sharp, being creative and focusing on something that means a lot to you is a great way to add an inexpensive self-care routine to your already busy day. Reading can help you unwind and learn something new at the same time.
- Spend quality time with your family. During the chaos, I missed out on a lot of great moments. Don't allow the pressure and stress, whether created by someone else, take you away from what's most important. Allow your family to help you de-stress.
- Meditate. Guided directed thought is a great way to calm yourself and reduce negativity that might try to seep in your life. Meditation helps to reduce stress, improve your health and sleep. It also helps slow down the aging process.
- Take a class. Learning something new is always great.

- Speak to a therapist. Talking to someone who won't judge you can be an awesome benefit. Not to mention, your friends and family might get stressed listening to your stress.
- Hug someone. There is scientific proof that hugging boosts oxytocin and serotonin levels. Not only that, when received by the right people (you know, that whole energy exchange thing) they are so amazing and just feel great!
- Take on a new hobby. Again, never stop learning.
- Join a fitness class. More importantly, commit to your health and wellness. If joining a class will get you up and moving- then do it.
- Hold hands with your significant other. Science, again, shares that it boosts bonds and is a great stress reliever. Holding hands, with someone you love, can make you feel secure. It's one of those nonverbal communication tools that lets the other person know that you care and that they are loved.
- Be sure to take vitamins and herbal supplements. There are so many benefits to taking your vitamins. Simply put, it

improves your skin, memory, aging, stress, strength and nutritional deficiencies, to name a few.

The point is to keep (and have) options that will add to your self-care regimen. Do the things that are meaningful to you. When times get rough, as they do, don't shut out the people who you love and those who love you. Take care of yourself. Have several plans.

While the following list of people are located in the Metropolitan Atlanta area, be sure to seek out wellness modalities in your area. I choose to include this list based on *some* of the people who surrounded me, providing a service/support while I endured through the hell. Find your wellness team and keep them close. Taking care of yourself is important and necessary.

Resources:

Company	Contact	Services
Atlanta Center for Family Wellness	Dr. Nathaniel Wilson Phone Number: (404) 550-9981 AC4FW@Bellsouth.Net	*CHILD AND ADOLESCENT INTERVENTION, ADULT TREATMENT, SERVICES FOR COUPLES/FAMILIES, EXTENDED SERVICES/PROGRAMS*
Back to Serenity Massage	Clarissa "Serenity" Francis 2serene4stress@gmail.com IG & Twitter: @back2serenity	Massage Services and Wellness Education
Nzinga Felix	Info@Nzinga.biz www.Nzinga.biz 678.792.8483	Certified, School Counselor and Bully Prevention Specialist Certified Egyptian Yoga and Womb Yoga Instructor, Womb Wellness

Company	Contact	Services
SisterCARE Alliance	Anana Harris Parris, Founder sistercarealliance@gmail.com	
Skintrition Prescriptions	Amina Nicole, Licensed Esthetician AminaNicole@skintritionprescriptions.com	Skin Care Products
SweetSpot Vtox Boutique, Atlanta	Aje'Wu-Ra, Executive Visionary www.sweetspotatlanta.com (404) 585-6351	Womb Wellness, Spirit Speaker, Inner Health and Wellness LyfeStyle Coach

Research/Materials to Further Look Into:

- Nethels, S. (2010). The Principal's Role in Creating and Maintaining Working Conditions in Schools in Georgia.
- National Center for Educational Statistics (Table 211.60) https://nces.ed.gov/programs/digest/d13/tables/dt13_211.60.asp
- The Inventory of Principals 'Characteristics that Contribute to Teacher Empowerment (IPCCTE).
- "Education: The Moral Imperative" by Dr. Adelaide Sanford. This is a transcript of the keynote address given by Dr. Sanford at a school development program principals academy.
- **DVD:** "I Am a Promise: The Children of Stanton Elementary School" a film by Alan and Susan Raymond

A wise person will always find a way. ~ Tanzanian proverb

Epilogue: "…It is lightened."

Why call this "*100 Days of Hell?*" Yes, of course there are more than one hundred days in the school calendar. When I thought it was a good idea to begin documenting this experience, the school year had begun and we had more days in front of us than we had behind us. I had long begun to count the days down through the next break and even through the last day of school. I truly didn't foresee going through so many days, enduring the grueling pursuit of having to protect my character.

Upon completing this body of work, I was surprised that there were 105 days in which I wrote/journaled about the events that were occurring. I had come up with the title for the book midway through its creation. I figured editing the small details and some of the insignificant happenings would even out the manuscript, making it one hundred days. After editing, I found more journal entries and decided to keep them, even if it took me beyond the titles namesake. It was important to keep those details.

Often, I was able to keep up with the rigmarole of the day by writing throughout the day and sometimes releasing at night. It was cathartic, the release. However, one hundred days of anything is quite a long time. To go through more than one hundred days, in a place of hell truly changed me. Some have expressed that it takes 21 days to create a habit…but no one really knows how long it takes to create a monster. In those one hundred plus days, I became somewhat of a monster. Unknown (and unrecognizable at times) to myself and to those who know me, but a monster ready to battle what was put in front of me.

There is no esoteric meaning for the name of the book, as it could have easily been called "*105 Days of Hell,*" or any number one deems worthy or catastrophic enough to capture what was endured.

As for the hell part, Merriam-Webster defines hell as a place or state of misery, torment or wickedness. I was in a place where wickedness abounded. It was a hellish state, in my life, in my profession. In addition to the literal definition, many feel that hell is an eternal state and because of the way my professional environment was impacting my personal life I felt that what I was going through had the potential to be eternal. Every decision I made (or didn't make) affected me and could conceivably have long term consequences. At one point, my family relationships were deteriorating, my health was getting worse and I risked losing my certifications. I didn't know how (or if) I would get out of this hell without being in a situation that affected me for the rest of my life.

Hell, a state of misery, a "stage in life, mentally, physically, emotionally (or otherwise), where a person meets extreme difficulty, challenges and oppression." My emotions were challenged; extreme anxiety, anger and frustration to name a few. My physical being was challenged; my health began to take a toll, to the point that I was prescribed medication to maintain in a stressful environment. My mentality was challenged, I felt like a madwoman. There were times where I wanted to do physical harm to this thing of an administrator. I considered damaging or blowing up her car. I even thought of following her home and hurting her. That's not even in my character, yet I had all those feelings. It was a stage in life that was hell, created from my environment.

I chose to channel those feelings and do something about it—even if it's as simple as awareness. During that time, I chose to fight the systematic flow of how things were conducted at this school. I chose to show up in a way that she may not have expected and be very vocal about it within the means that were available to me as an educator. Who knows if any or all of these things were a factor in her being demoted and placed in a different school. I'd like to think that the noise made, forced a level of change. Now, as a certified *Bullying Prevention Specialist* with the American School Counseling Association (ASCA), I am focusing on advocating for children who experience bullying as well as bringing awareness to the voiceless adults who are harassed through workplace bullying.

Although she is in a different school, as an assistant principal, I cannot help but think of the people in which she infected along the way. Yes, infected through venomous poison, deceit, manipulation and unfair treatment. I cannot help but think of all the children who had to endure her "leadership" and the many teachers we lost because of a failed school and her failed leadership. I cannot help but wonder if she is still bringing destruction in covert ways—

because I know she is still unhappy and miserable. I cannot help but wonder why this school system failed us all.

Made in the USA
Columbia, SC
02 August 2017